print *at the* CORONET

presents

A BREAKFAST
OF EELS

by Robert Holman

A Breakfast of Eels received its world premiere at
Print Room at the Coronet on 20 March 2015

A BREAKFAST OF EELS

by Robert Holman

Francis	Andrew Sheridan
Penrose Collins	Matthew Tennyson

Director	Robert Hastie
Designer	Ben Stones
Lighting Designer	Nicholas Holdridge
Sound Designer	George Dennis
Assistant Director	Jez Pike

Production Manager	Andy Beardmore
Stage Manager	Sophie Goody
Technical Stage Manager	Charlotte Oliver
Design Placement	Danielle Dent-Davis
Stage Management Placement	Sean Edwards
Scenic Painter	Natasha Shepherd
Set Builder	Andy Stubbs
Singing Tutor	Danny Standing
Production Photography	Nobby Clark

Special thanks to Donmar Warehouse, Hampstead Theatre, Playground Theatre

Biographies

Andrew Sheridan, Francis

Andrew's theatre credits include *Blindsided, Being Friends, Antigone, Jonah and Otto, Across Oka, The Rise and Fall of Little Voice*, and *Port* (Manchester Royal Exchange); *Henry VI, parts 1, 2 & 3* (Shakespeare's Globe); *One Day When We Were Young, The Sound of Heavy Rain* (Paines Plough's London Roundabout season); *A Thousand Stars Explode in the Sky* (Lyric Hammersmith); and *Holes in the Skin* (Chichester Minerva Theatre).

Television credits include *Peaky Blinders, The Trials of Jimmy Rose, Home Front, Heartbeat, Coronation Street, Kingdom, Cold Blood, Shameless, Buried, Night Flight, Urban Gothic* and *Clocking Off*, and on film, *Control*.

Andrew's first play *Winterlong* won the 2008 Bruntwood Playwriting Competition and premiered at the Royal Exchange Theatre in Manchester before transferring to the Soho Theatre. The play has been translated and performed across Europe. At the moment he is on attachment to the National Theatre Studio.

Matthew Tennyson, Penrose Collins

Matthew trained at LAMDA before making his West End debut in *Flare Path* at the Theatre Royal Haymarket directed by Trevor Nunn. His other theatre credits include *Beautiful Thing* (Manchester Royal Exchange; Manchester Theatre Award, Best Newcomer); *Making Noise Quietly* (Donmar Warehouse; Evening Standard Theatre Award, Outstanding Newcomer); and Puck in *A Midsummer Night's Dream* (Shakespeare's Globe).

Television credits include *Babylon, Humans, The Borgias* and *The Hollow Crown*. On film, credits include *Pride*. Radio credits include *Jonesy, Pilgrim* and *Homefront*.

Robert Holman, Writer

Robert Holman is one of the celebrated playwrights of the British Theatre. His plays include: *German Skerries* (Bush Theatre, 1977); *Other Worlds* (Royal Court Theatre, 1980); *Today* (Royal Shakespeare Company, 1984); *The Overgrown Path* (Royal Court Theatre, 1985); *Making Noise Quietly* (Bush Theatre, 1987); *Across Oka* (Royal Shakespeare Company, 1988); *Rafts and Dreams* (Royal Court Theatre, 1990); *Bad Weather* (Royal Shakespeare Company, 1998); *Holes in the Skin* (Chichester Festival Theatre, 2003); *Jonah and Otto* (Royal Exchange Theatre, 2008) and *A Thousand Stars Explode in the Sky*, co-written with David Eldridge and Simon Stephens (Lyric Theatre, Hammersmith, 2010). His play *Making Noise Quietly* was revived at the Donmar Warehouse in 2012, and *Jonah and Otto* at the Park Theatre in 2014.

Robert has also written a novel, *The Amish Landscape*.

Robert Hastie, Director

Robert studied English at Cambridge and trained as an actor at Rada. He is Associate Director of the Donmar Warehouse, where he directed Kevin Elyot's *My Night with Reg*, which recently transferred to the Apollo Theatre and earned Robert a nomination for the Evening Standard Award for Emerging Talent.

Other directing credits include: *Carthage* by Chris Thompson (Finborough Theatre); *The Hotel Plays: Sunburst* by Tennessee Williams (Defibrillator); *Events While Guarding the Bofors Gun* by John McGrath (Finborough Theatre); *In the Land of Uz* by Neil LaBute, *The Middle Man* by Anthony Weigh, *David and Goliath* by Andrew Motion, *Snow in Sheffield* by Helen Mort, and *A Lost Expression* by Luke Kennard (all part of the Sixty-Six Books season at the Bush Theatre, for which he was also Associate Director).

Ben Stones, Designer

Designs include: *Good With People* by David Harrower (Paines Plough and 59E59 NYC); *Creditors* directed by Alan Rickman, translation by David Greig (Donmar Warehouse/BAM New York); *The Kitchen Sink* (Bush Theatre); *Belong, Ingredient X* (Royal Court Theatre Upstairs); *Thom Pain (based on nothing)* (Print Room); *No Idea* (Improbable Theatre at Young Vic); *Kiss of the Spider Woman* (Donmar Warehouse); *An Enemy of the People*, *Kes* (dance-theatre premiere; Sheffield Crucible); *Paradise Lost* (Headlong Theatre); *The Mighty Boosh* (national tour); *Still Game: Live!* (Hydro Arena, Glasgow); *Speaking in Tongues* (Duke of York's Theatre); *The Lady in the Van* (national tour); *The Painter* (Arcola Theatre); *Doctor Faustus, Edward II, A Taste of Honey* (Royal Exchange); *Some Like It Hip Hop* (Sadler's Wells/national tour); *My Generation* (West Yorkshire Playhouse); *Groove On Down the Road* (QEH Southbank Centre); *ZooNation Unplugged* (Sadler's Wells); *Burberry: London in Shanghai* (Shanghai); *The Mad Hatter's Tea Party* (Royal Opera House); *Hobson's Choice, Twelfth Night* (Regent's Park Open Air Theatre).

Short films include: *Holloway Launderette*, written and choreographed by Kate Prince (Bafta Dance Commision), and the Frank McGuinness premiere of *Crocodile* for Sky Arts Live.

Awards include: MEN 2011 Award for Best Design for *Doctor Faustus* at the Royal Exchange.

Nicholas Holdridge, Lighting Designer
Theatre includes: *Between Us* (Arcola Theatre); *Events While Guarding the Bofors Gun* (Finborough Theatre; short-listed for Best Lighting Designer by Off West End Awards 2013); *The Hotel Plays* (Grange Hotel Holborn/Defibrillator); *Deathwatch, House of Bones, Till Death us do Part, The Criminals* (Drama Centre London); *Billy the Kid, Buttons, The Three Musketeers, Beowulf! The Panto* (Charles Court Opera); *Sense and Sensibility* (Rosemary Branch/ Yvonne Arnauld, Guildford); *Memory Cells* (Hannah Eidinow/ Pleasance); *Scott Mills The Musical* (BBC Radio 1/Pleasance); *Immodesty Blaize and Walter's Burlesque!* (Arts Theatre); *Everybody Look at Me, Bones* (FifthWord Theatre); *The Tempest* (TARA Arts); *The Promise* (Mercury Theatre Colchester); *Much Ado About Nothing, A Midsummer Night's Dream* (Mercury Theatre Colchester Youth Theatre); *Uncle Vanya, Wink the Other Eye, Immodesty Blaize and the Adventures of Walter, The Spotted Cow and the Piano Forte* (Wilton's Music Hall). Previous dance includes: *The Firebird* (English National Ballet); *A Single Act, Yellow Card* (Khamlane Halsackda); *Inside Out, Rush, Silent Steps* (Pair Dance) and as 'Festival Designer' for Cloud Dance Festival, 2010–2013. Previous opera and operetta includes *La Gioconda, Edgar* (Feria De Valladolid); *La Bohème, The Pirates of Penzance, Patience, Ruddigore, The Mikado, The Zoo, Trial by Jury* (Charles Court Opera); *Don Giovanni, Xerxes* (Iford Arts); *The Yeomen of the Guard* (Buxton Opera House).

George Dennis, Sound Designer
Theatre includes: *Beautiful Thing* (West End/UK tour); *Fireworks, Liberian Girl* (Royal Court Theatre); *peddling* (Arcola Theatre/ 59E59, New York/HighTide Festival); *Visitors* (Bush Theatre); *The Edge of our Bodies, Dances of Death* (Gate Theatre); *Regeneration* (Royal & Derngate/UK tour); *Mametz* (National Theatre of Wales); *Minotaur* (Polka Theatre/Clwyd Theatr Cymru); *Spring Awakening* (Headlong Theatre); *The Island* (Young Vic); *Love Your Soldiers* (Sheffield Crucible Studio); *The Last Yankee* (Print Room); *Thark* (Park Theatre); *Moth* (Bush Theatre/HighTide Festival); *Hello/ Goodbye* (Hampstead Theatre); *Liar Liar* (Unicorn Theatre); *Good Grief* (Theatre Royal Bath/UK tour); *The Seven Year Itch* (Salisbury Playhouse); *When Did You Last See My Mother?* (Trafalgar Studios 2); *The Living Room* (Jermyn Street Theatre); *Debris, The Seagull, The Only True History of Lizzie Finn* (Southwark Playhouse); *A Life, Foxfinder* (Finborough Theatre).

print room
at the CORONET

The Print Room was founded in 2010 by Artistic Director Anda Winters, in a converted printing workshop in Notting Hill. Over the last five years, the intimate West London theatre has built a reputation for producing and curating a highly acclaimed and varied programme of performance and visual arts, including theatre, dance, music, exhibitions and multidisciplinary collaborations, in a friendly and welcoming environment.

Recent highlights include the UK premieres of Howard Barker's *Lot and His God* and Jon Fosse's *The Dead Dogs*, the world premieres of new contemporary dance commissions *FLOW* (set in water) and *IGNIS* (inspired by Fire), the major revivals of Brian Friel's *Molly Sweeney* and Will Eno's *Thom Pain (based on nothing)*, experimental art/opera *Triptych*, live-art performance Alice Anderson's *Travelling Factory*, as well as the re-imagination of modern classics such as Harold Pinter's *The Dumb Waiter*, Arthur Miller's *The Last Yankee* and the award-winning production of *Uncle Vanya*.

When developers took over the original Print Room building in 2014, the charity moved to its new permanent home, Notting Hill's the Coronet, where it opened its doors for the company's inaugural autumn season in October 2014 to present the first theatrical performance in the Coronet for nearly a century.

The Coronet began life as a Victorian playhouse back in 1898 and later became a legendary cinema. The Print Room will restore the iconic venue in stages, to take the space back to its theatrical roots whilst improving its cinema facilities.

Over the next three years, the Print Room's ambitions will expand as the main auditorium is reopened, alongside the flexible studio theatre, to bring world-class cinema on 35mm and new digital facilities to its audience.

This will allow the building to offer cross-arts programming between the two major spaces whilst continuing to create work with emerging and established artists from all fields.

Print Room at the Coronet, 103 Notting Hill Gate, London, W11 3LB
www.the-print-room.org | 020 3642 6606

The Print Room is generously supported by

Corporate Sponsors

markit®

Markit are match-funders and supporters of the Print Room
outreach ticket scheme.
Autonomous Research
Studio Indigo

Headline
Allen Fisher Foundation, Clive & Helena Butler, Paolo &
Aud Cuniberti, Mike Fisher, Roderick & Elizabeth Jack,
Amanda Waggott

Capital
Anon, Ben & Louisa Brown, Glenda Burkhart, Matt Cooper,
John & Jennifer Crompton, Ayelet Elstein, Lara Fares,
Connie Freeman, Ashish Goyal, Tom & Maarit Glocer,
Julian Granville & Louisiana Lush, Debbie Hannam, Anne
Herd, Posgate Charitable Trust, The Ruddick Foundation
for the Arts, Alison Winter

Bold
John & Laura Banes, Bill Reeves & Debbie Berger, Tony
& Kate Best, Bruno & Christiane Boesch, Caroline & Ian
Cormack, Victoria Gray, Cecile Guillon, Isabelle Hotimsky,
Martin Jacomb, Kristen Kennish, Amy Lashinsky, David
Leathers, Jonathan Levy, Tony Mackintosh, Matt & Amanda
McEvoy, Julia Rochester, Lois Sieff, Rita Skinner, Antony
Thomlinson, Vahiria Vedet Janbon, Pamela Williams

Special thanks to: Aki Ando, Mimi Gilligan, Louisa Lane Fox

A BREAKFAST OF EELS

Robert Holman

An Introduction of sorts from Robert Holman

I am writing these words with the strange sense of something that was finished is now to begin again. I can't pin down the feeling and give a name to it. I care too much about my work for this to be easy. A play stays in a kind of limbo until an actor speaks the words, when everything changes. We begin rehearsing my new play in a week's time. The better the actor the more I'm going to be hurt by them. A fine production will dig its teeth in and not let go. There is pain in the writing and the putting on of plays that has to be savoured, if you are me, and generosities to be given out. The play is to belong to other people and cease to be mine alone. If I have one hope it's this: at some point fairly soon, perhaps in a quiet corner during a dress rehearsal, I will marvel that I had anything to do with the play at all and burst into tears. The play as I lived it in my imagination, spent hours with it for months on end, will be gone for ever.

I'm not a father, so if fathers will forgive me and if it isn't too pompous, this is the nearest I come to the birth of a child. I know plays are not as important as children.

A Breakfast of Eels, like most things I've written, began as a doodle on scrap paper. I like scrap paper because it's not serious and can be thrown away. I learnt a long time ago not to put too much pressure on myself. In my late twenties (I'm sixty-two now) I got it into my head that I had to write a great play, and so didn't write anything for three years. I also like scrap paper because it's not clever and I start to worry when the pile runs down, because it means a play is coming into my head. My plays are worried over. About every third doodle I get past the scrap-paper stage and move onto a notepad, in ink. It's hard not to think too much and to write the next line, but that is some of my effort. I don't decide my plays, my plays decide me. If they have any power at all, it's the power of learning and of the energy that can come out of a newly found thought.

I know this is an unfashionable way to write, but to care too much about fashion, which by its nature comes and goes, is to be a fool. In messing about on bits of paper I'm not being modest, because I have an arrogance that wants to at least try to understand and explain the world as it changes. To not care too much about fashion is a beautiful thing.

Some of this doodling nonsense was in my head as I sat with Matthew Tennyson on a bright spring afternoon in a café in Covent Garden. He was appearing in my play *Making Noise Quietly* in a theatre round the corner. I'm also a liar and a cheat. At home, often late at night on a desk littered in paper, I had begun to wonder if I could write for him. To try to write for an actor is a slow and careful process. On a simple level, the actor may be hurt if I throw the paper away, so, in some of the first sunshine of the year, as if I didn't have a care in the world, I got him to talk about the theatre and parts he might want to play, and I tried to listen with all the power that listening can have. To want to write for an actor is really to want to listen to them. And to be challenged by what is heard. I paid for the tea and his cake, and he, none-the-wiser, went off to work in a play I'd seen many times. His performance had been making me think again.

Andrew Sheridan was also swimming about my brain. I'd written for him before. My play *Jonah and Otto* belongs to him. I was writing down his name, along with Tennyson's, in the left margin of the paper. The names of my characters are crucial to me. I have characters change sex, old characters become young and vice-versa. The great thing about a doodle is that it has no laws. Names can change at the drop of a hat. When I get a name and it stays, it means I'm beginning to get a character. Jonah is a name Sheridan came up with. When he said it, I thought to myself quietly: 'Help. Help.' (A pause.) 'I can't write a Jonah.' But I had asked him for the name of a character he might like to play. If we ask a question, then we must be open to the reply. With a name comes all sorts of connotations and feelings. On the paper, in the left margin, I began to switch all the names written there to Jonah, and Jonah began to emerge. He was a character I never would have written had Sheridan not said what he did.

When *Making Noise Quietly* was over, Tennyson and I went for a walk along the Thames. I said how, now and again, I'd had a go at writing parts for actors and would he be interested if I was to write a play for him, and that at some point I would need the name of his character. The only thing I knew for certain was that I wanted the play to be set in London (Tennyson is a Londoner) and would he show me his favourite part of London? Most of my plays are set in the north of England (I was brought up in North Yorkshire) but when I go back now I get lost. I've decided not to write about the place any more. We must have walked ten miles that afternoon in the drizzle without an umbrella. He said he would show me Highgate Cemetery, and a few days later said 'Penrose'. Penrose is a character I never would have written had Tennyson not said what he did.

To me writing is a practical thing. It's something I try to do. There are good days and bad days. On good days I hear and see people moving about a stage; on bad days it's just frustrating. I've never worked out why some days are good and others are bad. I do know the good days have to increase if I'm to find the confidence to finish a play, when the bad days become useful. To have a bad day then is to learn to trust a good day. Trust plays an enormous part in writing. When I read great plays I somehow know the writer trusted themselves, and they dig deep. They go into the places that hurt. Some of this is innate, some of it is learnt, but all of it takes a single mind, one that refuses to apologise, and courage. And all writers tell lies.

A small bird has just hit my window. In the garden it looked more like a piece of coal than a thing with feathers, but I put it in a box and took it up the road to the vet. I'm reminded of the story Francis frightens Penrose with in *A Breakfast of Eels* about eating the chaffinch. I wonder if we should believe him in this instance and why he says it.

Sheridan has a way with stories. He will ring me up and tell me something outlandish has happened, make it completely plausible, and then tell me he's pulling my leg. I've tried to become wise to this, but always fail. Time and again he succeeds. In these moments I always forget he's an actor and is acting. At other times we might talk about what acting is, about how an actor has to live through the moment and not know what his character is going to do next, whilst, at the same time, watching themselves doing it. It's a paradox I didn't completely understand at first until I realised it's very similar to the way I write.

I asked Sheridan if there was anything he wanted to do (I could at least try to put it in) in the new play, and he replied that he'd like to wear clothes that were too big, if possible, and to sing. Funnily enough (they hadn't yet met at this stage) Tennyson had also told me he would like to sing when I asked him the same question. He had added that singing is really exposing. It was a moment filled with vulnerability and honesty, and I was excited to think about his character singing, if also a little scared. Could I write a play where a character sang? What did it mean if a character was to wear clothes that were too big? The actor can put these things in my imagination, but I have to make them real. As is the way with a fairground ride, I felt exhilarated yet also scared. Just as I won't go on a roller-coaster unless pushed on, if I were to do what the actors suggested I would have to go into areas where I would not normally and naturally go. This is the great thing about writing for actors.

Tennyson had taken me around Highgate Cemetery (I'd been back several times on my own) and we met there again, one Sunday afternoon, with Sheridan. Once more it was raining. To say it was an important moment underestimates it for the three of us. It was the first time they had met. It was the first time I had seen them together. For the first time I could listen to their voices one after the other. I told them I thought the doodles and notepad had come good and that there was going to be a play. I showed them one particular grave where there was a pot filled with pens and pencils, and said I intended to steal the idea because it was very Penrose and Francis. I explained as best as I could, as much as I knew, about some of the action of the play, but that there was still much to find out about the two characters and why they had started to do what they were doing. I said I was reasonably confident Francis and Penrose would become independent of me, teach me, tell me about their lives, and become real. In the same way I said Penrose and Francis had to become independent of them as people because I was trying to write characters they could act. The play had to be bigger than the three of us.

The devil comes into me when I write. The vet has just rung to say he thinks the bird was shocked and will recover. For some reason, I'm reminded of Francis and the responsibilities he carries. His sister died under the stairs when he was a boy. He has no reason to feel guilty but he does. Penrose manages finally to get him to talk about it. I don't know why this is important to anyone else except these two people, or what I write about. I was going to say something about London, but have I? And the courage it can take to behave responsibly and well. I was going to try to write about what it is to be a man, and about money. Have I done any of these things and more? As history is the judge of almost everything, so history is the judge of plays and will be of this one.

The final draft of *A Breakfast of Eels* was written on a twelve-year-old keypad at the computer, but I can come up with dialogue whilst buying the milk so have paper in my pocket and almost everywhere else. So much of the play was still in my head. The challenge is to put it down, line by line, whilst still being open to its moments changing. Sometimes the characters in a play will not do what I would like them to do, but I always go with them. For this play, pinned on the wall, so I could turn and look at them when I got stuck, were photographs of Highgate Village, Northumberland, Parliament Hill and the two actors who I was trying to see in these places playing Penrose and Francis. In Highgate Francis produced a buttonhole for Penrose which surprised me. On Parliament Hill they talked about serious things and Penrose had a box of chocolates. And a year later in the play it started snowing. Line by next line the play was done and shed, until there was nothing left to see and hear and think about.

I gave the first two copies of *A Breakfast of Eels*, printed on watermarked paper, to Tennyson and Sheridan, and waited nervously to hear from them.

The relationship between a writer and a director is the most important one in the theatre. I could argue that this is the case even if the writer has been dead for centuries. Rob Hastie read the play. Would he be interested in directing it? We met in a muddy Highgate Cemetery (where else?) and walked round it three times. He was sensible and wearing boots, whereas I was more Penrose in Northumberland and had put on soft shoes. I explained how I thought the play had to go on in a normal way despite its genesis. It was a play written for two actors, but that I would have failed them and let them down if the play could not, at some point in the future, be done by others. I said how Sheridan and Tennyson were capable of playing many more colours than I could write for, and would he help them to find some of those extra colours and so take the play away from me? A short while later the four of us met in Notting Hill, and a little while after this he said he would like to direct the play.

I have been asked if Sheridan and Tennyson are my muse. I've looked up the word in a dictionary (as Francis looks up words) and still don't quite understand the question. I know they will do what I write and more, however contradictory, naughty and unfathomable it is to begin with. I could write 'He swings upside down on a chandelier with a monkey in his mouth', and both of them would do it. But the truth is I prefer smaller things, such as that he makes a bow and arrow or reads in silence. My plays need actors to be brave. It takes a braver actor to read in silence than it does to swing from a chandelier. To write for these two actors gives me a kind of freedom (the word muse has an arty-farty nonsense about it) – and to be free is why I write. And I think it's why they act. We share the same courage.

A Breakfast of Eels was written for Matthew Tennyson and Andrew Sheridan. I'm a pest, and would like to thank them both for their intelligence and tolerance during the months of its writing.

February 2015

Characters

FRANCIS
PENROSE COLLINS

The play is set in the present day in Highgate, London, and
Northumberland. There is one interval.

A Note on the Songs

In Act One Penrose sings 'Silent Worship' by George Frideric
Handel. In Act Two Penrose plays on the piano, and he and
Francis sing 'Fields of Athenry' by Pete St John. In Act Five
Penrose plays 'A Day in the Life' by Lennon/McCartney which
drifts into 'Love' by John Lennon, and later sings the aria *'J'ai
perdu mon Eurydice'* from the opera *Orphée et Eurydice* by
Christoph Willibald Gluck. In subsequent productions this may
be different. The songs tell a story.

*This text went to press before the end of rehearsals and so may
differ slightly from the play as performed.*

ACT ONE

The vast lawn at 2 Old Highgate Road, London. The shadows of apple trees are being cast by the morning sun. It is late summer. As if thrown onto the grass are hundreds of apples, brought down by a storm in the night, and a few boxes, some with apples already in them and some not. There is a wasp trapped in an empty jam jar.

FRANCIS, *aged thirty-five, is eating toast. He is dressed in a black suit at least two sizes too big, a white shirt and polished, black shoes. He licks his fingers clean. He picks up apples and puts them in a box.*

PENROSE COLLINS *is twenty-one. He is wearing jeans, a white T-shirt, a grey jumper with holes in it, and soft shoes with the laces unfastened.*

PENROSE (*entering, doing a skip and a jump*). I had blackberries for breakfast. (*A hop.*) I had them in a teacup. (*A skip.*) They tasted of tea. (*A jump.*) Which was a waste of the blackberries.

He does a hop and a skip, stops by the jam jar and bends over to look at it.

What's this here?

FRANCIS. What does it look like?

PENROSE. A wasp in a jam jar.

FRANCIS. That's what it is then.

PENROSE *looks at* FRANCIS *for a moment.*

PENROSE. Why are you wearing one of Daddy's suits?

FRANCIS. I thought I would today. Daddy doesn't need it any longer. (*Stops picking up apples.*) Your hair looks like birds are nesting in it. Why aren't you bathed? Why aren't you dressed? Why aren't you ready to go?

PENROSE (*combing his hair with his fingers*). No, I am bathed.

A slight pause.

FRANCIS. We've Daddy's funeral this morning.

PENROSE. Yes.

A slight pause.

(*Doing a hop.*) Why should I want to see Daddy when he's put in the soil? (*Doing a skip.*) He's not a tree. (*A jump.*) Pluto's under the weather.

FRANCIS. He had a furball.

PENROSE. Hairball, actually.

FRANCIS. Whatever it is cats get, he won't miss you this morning.

A slight pause.

PENROSE. No.

FRANCIS. I'll miss you, Penrose.

A slight pause.

PENROSE. Yes. (*Bending down to fasten one of his shoelaces.*) I stayed here when you put Mummy in the ground. I was only eleven. I watched you all go with my forehead on a window at the top of the house. It was raining the sort of infuriating rain that makes you damp rather than wet.

FRANCIS. Drizzle.

PENROSE. Yes.

A slight pause.

FRANCIS. You're going to Daddy's funeral if I have to drag you into a suit myself.

PENROSE *gulps and* FRANCIS *picks up apples.*

PENROSE (*doing a hop, suddenly singing*).
    Did you not hear my lady
    go down the garden singing?

A skip.

> Blackbird and thrush were silent
> to hear the alleys ringing

A jump.

> O saw you not my lady
> out in the garden there?

A hop.

> Shaming the rose and lily
> for she is twice as fair

He is still.

> Though I am nothing to her
> though she must rarely look at me
> and though I could never woo her
> I love her till I die

FRANCIS. I'll break your legs into small pieces if you don't go and get ready.

PENROSE *gulps.*

PENROSE (*doing a skip*).
> Surely you heard my lady
> go down the garden singing?

A jump.

> Silencing all the songbirds
> and setting the alleys ringing

A hop.

> But surely you see my lady
> out in the garden there

A skip.

> Rivalling the glittering sunshine
> with a glory of golden hair.

He picks up an apple and holds it out as a peace offering.

A slight pause.

FRANCIS *comes over. He spits on the apple.* PENROSE *flinches.*

A slight pause.

PENROSE *wipes the apple clean with a handkerchief and offers it to* FRANCIS *again.* FRANCIS *takes it and puts it in a box. He picks up apples.* PENROSE *watches him.*

(*Twisting the neck of his jumper.*) I don't know why I've not told you before, Francis, but I'm definitely not going to Daddy's funeral. I understand it's remiss of me. It just isn't convenient today.

FRANCIS. You've more excuses than the present politicians.

PENROSE. I shan't pussyfoot about. I've things here to be busy with.

FRANCIS. Why should I go on my own?

PENROSE. Well, I think you're rather excellent on these occasions.

A slight pause.

FRANCIS. There will be hundreds of mourners at the church, I've no doubt.

PENROSE. Yes.

FRANCIS. All looking out for you.

A slight pause.

PENROSE. No.

FRANCIS. All wondering where you are.

A slight pause.

PENROSE. No.

FRANCIS. Daddy was an influential man, which makes it significant for you. It's going to be an immense occasion.

PENROSE (*quietly*). Help.

A slight pause.

Why am I so insanely worthless?

FRANCIS. You're not worthless, certainly not today. If I have to drag you by your hair you're going.

PENROSE *gulps*.

PENROSE. I dearly wish I wasn't so worthless.

FRANCIS (*taking a black tie from his pocket and putting it on*). Penrose, the cars will be here in exactly ten minutes.

PENROSE (*doing a hop*). Why should I want Daddy in the soil attacked by armies of hungry worms?

FRANCIS. You won't see it.

PENROSE (*doing a skip*). Yes, but I've an imagination. (*A jump.*) Was Mummy eaten by ravenous bugs?

FRANCIS. You know she was buried.

PENROSE. Yes, why in heaven did I ask? (*Bends down to fasten the other shoelace.*) I was so completely flummoxed by it all when she vanished. I actually believe you're wearing the same tie. We went along to see her a week or two later. You absolutely insisted I see her grave... and took my hand as we stood by the headstone you and Daddy had arranged in her memory. It was a misty day... you wept, copiously.

FRANCIS. It was a long time ago. Ten years have gone by at the speed of light.

PENROSE. Why are you angry?

FRANCIS. I'm not angry in the slightest. I'm very frustrated.

PENROSE. I could wear those horrible red trousers I bought by mistake when I was feeling silly and euphoric, not my usual self at all. And purchase a yellow jacket to go with them which I can shop for after lunch. I could go as a rainbow.

FRANCIS *fiddles with the collar of his shirt*.

FRANCIS. Penrose, you wept that afternoon, didn't you?

PENROSE *nods slightly*.

I cried because you did. I was doing my best to be really strong for your sake.

PENROSE. Yes.

FRANCIS. This isn't fair. You're not being fair at all. Go and put a suit on before I do get angry.

PENROSE. You misunderstand me, Francis. My point is… it's the only time I've ever seen you cry.

FRANCIS (*slightly angrily*). Does it matter a fig at this moment?

PENROSE. Yes.

FRANCIS. Why?

PENROSE. Mummy and Daddy are gone and we're by ourselves… it's a memory I cherish.

FRANCIS. I give up, I surrender. The fight is over. I pay homage to your tenacity.

FRANCIS sits on the grass. PENROSE starts to sit down.

Don't you sit down.

PENROSE does as he is told and gets up quickly.

I just can't be as obdurate as you. I wish I could.

PENROSE picks up an apple to put in a box.

Don't do that either.

PENROSE carefully puts the apple on the grass.

PENROSE. We'll have to give them away free, like we did last year, in a box on the pavement. I'll never comprehend why you planted so many trees.

He is uncomfortable and plays with his fingers.

FRANCIS. Penrose, please. Please behave.

PENROSE looks at his watch for a long time and fiddles with the strap.

(*Quietly.*) I'll leave you.

PENROSE. Pardon?

FRANCIS. I think that's what I'll do.

A slight pause.

I'll be free.

A slight pause.

PENROSE (*quietly*). Help.

FRANCIS. I'll go. You won't see hide or hair of me again.

PENROSE. Help.

A slight pause.

FRANCIS. I'll disappear.

A slight pause.

When everything is done and dusted today, you will not see
me again.

A slight pause.

PENROSE. Help.

A slight pause.

We're brothers, Francis.

FRANCIS. We're not brothers when you behave in this way.
We're not brothers full stop at the moment. When you carry
on like this we're enemies.

A slight pause.

PENROSE. Yes.

FRANCIS. Help is something that's reciprocated.

PENROSE. Yes.

FRANCIS *gets to his feet.* PENROSE *wanders away and
hides his eyes.*

FRANCIS. Sulking won't help the minutes go slower.

PENROSE. I'm not sulking. (*Taking his handkerchief from his
pocket.*) I'm worrying quite profoundly. (*Wipes his eyes.*)
I've got your spit all over me now.

The hearse and a car pull into the drive not far away. They turn at the sound of the engines.

Oh hell. It's Daddy. He's utterly surrounded by exquisite white flowers.

FRANCIS. Yes.

FRANCIS *goes to him.*

PENROSE. It's heavenly. (*Catching his breath.*) Help. Did you arrange the flowers from the garden?

FRANCIS. Who else did it, Pen?

PENROSE. The roses are insanely beautiful.

FRANCIS. I picked them last night when the scent was at its most perfect. I did ask you.

PENROSE. My fault.

The engines are switched off.

Why am I useless?

A slight pause.

Why am I so pathetic?

A slight pause.

When will I learn to stand up for myself?

A slight pause.

FRANCIS. He's a few minutes early, Pen.

PENROSE. Yes.

PENROSE *goes slowly to the house.*

A slight pause.

FRANCIS *hears a piano being played in the music room.*

FRANCIS (*calling*). Penrose, not now.

The music stops.

A slight pause.

FRANCIS *picks up the jam jar. He looks at the wasp and picks up an apple. He takes off the lid. He squashes the apple into the jar and puts it on the grass.*

PENROSE *returns. His hair is combed. He is immaculately dressed in a dark suit, a white shirt, a tie, and black shoes. He is listening to music with an iPod.* FRANCIS *signals to him to take off the headphones.*

What are you listening to?

PENROSE. '*J'ai perdu mon Eurydice*' from the opera *Orphée et Eurydice.*

FRANCIS. Is it calming?

PENROSE. Yes, it is.

FRANCIS. Good.

PENROSE *sees the jam jar and goes over to it.*

PENROSE. What's happened here?

FRANCIS. An apple got in.

PENROSE *looks at* FRANCIS *for a moment.*

PENROSE. That was cruel, especially as I'm a vegetarian, and I once conducted a funeral for a wasp.

FRANCIS (*guiltily going away a few feet*). When you were seven you were stung on the cheek and went blue.

PENROSE. I forgave the wasp.

FRANCIS *picks up an apple and puts it in a box.*

FRANCIS. I remember the hullabaloo. (*Picking up the box and putting it down beside another one.*) I preferred you when you were seven and did everything topsy-turvy, sleep the wrong way in bed with your feet on the pillows.

PENROSE (*touching his lapel*). Daddy asked me to wear a flower. Are we wearing buttonholes?

FRANCIS. Yes.

FRANCIS *carefully takes a white rose from his jacket pocket and goes to him.* PENROSE *takes his hand and smells the flower.*

PENROSE. It's divine.

FRANCIS *puts the rose in his buttonhole.*

Where's yours?

FRANCIS *has another rose. He puts it in his own buttonhole.*

Did you know I'd agree to go?

FRANCIS. No. I didn't actually.

PENROSE. A murder and a funeral, all in the same morning. It's so fantastically difficult, Francis.

He looks at the hearse.

I'm not certain I want to be gawped at by hundreds of Daddy's friends, especially when I don't even know them.

He looks at FRANCIS.

I know I'm not what they expect.

A slight pause.

I'm a disappointment.

FRANCIS. Why don't you put your music on?

PENROSE (*shaking his head*). It's for a coward.

A slight pause.

Do you remember when I was asked to sing with the Bach Choir at Kenwood House? I was thirteen. Mummy was bones.

FRANCIS. Yes.

PENROSE. I sang two songs on my own with the orchestra. What's happened to me?

FRANCIS. You were a boy.

PENROSE. Why was I confident then and so flummoxed now?

FRANCIS. It's easier when we're boys.

PENROSE. Yes.

A slight pause.

Why can't I be sensible?

A slight pause.

FRANCIS. I remember your little curtsy at the end.

PENROSE. I bowed. Please. I bowed. I didn't curtsy.

FRANCIS. The thunderous applause brought you back on.

PENROSE. Don't exaggerate, please.

FRANCIS. Were you frightened?

PENROSE (*thinks for a moment*). I'd a butterfly in my tummy. Well, I couldn't sing now.

FRANCIS. Why?

PENROSE. I'd be too nervous. I know the dangers. I'm too timorous, I expect.

A slight pause.

FRANCIS. Daddy was proud of you.

PENROSE. Was he? He didn't mention it.

FRANCIS. He did in his lawyer's way.

PENROSE. Oh.

FRANCIS. He knew you were exceptional, Pen.

PENROSE *is embarrassed and looks down.*

Mummy would have known, too.

PENROSE. Would she?

FRANCIS. Yes.

A slight pause.

You were angelic, and looked about eight.

PENROSE. I didn't look about eight.

He looks at the hearse.

Was I as wonderful as the flowers?

FRANCIS. No, I wouldn't go as far as that.

A slight pause.

PENROSE. Will you hold my hand?

FRANCIS. No.

PENROSE. You always used to hold my hand whenever I asked.

FRANCIS. Yes.

A slight pause.

You go first.

PENROSE. Why?

FRANCIS. You go first. I'll be behind you. It's your day.

PENROSE *goes slowly towards the cars.* FRANCIS *follows him after a moment or two.*

ACT TWO

A year later.

The library at 2 Old Highgate Road. A wall of books, many of them decades old, about the law. There are also atlases and encyclopedias along with journals and biographies. There is an old writing desk. The leather top is crammed with family photographs in wooden and silver frames. A rug on the floor. The table lamps dotted about the room are switched on. There is a leather sofa and armchairs.

FRANCIS *is sprawled in one of them. His legs are over the armrest and he is reading about the law. He has glasses. He is dressed in jeans, a T-shirt and socks. There is a bottle of white wine and a glass of wine on the small table beside him. He drinks, concentrating on the book.*

PENROSE *enters. He is wearing black chinos, an old T-shirt worn at the collar, and socks. He has a glass of soft drink with a straw, and a paperback modern novel. He sits, more correctly than* FRANCIS, *in an armchair, finds his glasses in his pocket, and opens the book.*

FRANCIS. I thought you were having an early night?

PENROSE. So did I.

FRANCIS. What went wrong?

PENROSE. An early night didn't want to have me.

A pause.

(*Pretending he's reading.*) You're Tinkerbell. All I've seen is your shadow for weeks and weeks… months… a year, in point of fact.

A slight pause.

I've slowly cottoned on you're hiding in here… immersed in Daddy's books.

A slight pause.

Why don't you study for the bar and be a lawyer? It seems to me you're doing it already? I'd come along to listen to you, just as we would go and hear Daddy at the Old Bailey... occasionally.

He looks at his book. The two men read. Now and again one of them turns the page or absentmindedly scratches an itch. PENROSE *drinks through the straw. His thoughts are elsewhere and not on the book. They have been reading and not reading for two minutes.*

FRANCIS (*lifting his glasses*). All of Highgate heard you in the kitchen. Pans were flying hither and thither by the sound of it. What were you doing, chucking stuff about?

PENROSE. Well, very little, actually.

FRANCIS. I must teach you how to lie, remind me.

FRANCIS *reads.*

PENROSE. It's your birthday tomorrow.

FRANCIS. Is it? Another year bites the dust.

PENROSE. You once told me birthdays were illegal in the seventeenth century.

FRANCIS. I meant to say Christmas was illegal in the 1660s.

PENROSE (*quizzically*). I'm never quite certain about you. I told the boys at school and felt sorry for an entire century.

FRANCIS. Leave the kitchen reasonably tidy, Pen. It's not fair on Mrs Nicholson in the morning, or me getting my breakfast. And would you put her wages up, please. I used to remind Daddy every year.

PENROSE (*quietly*). Oh hell. Can't you do it, Francis?

FRANCIS. No. I can't do it this year. It's your responsibility.

PENROSE *plays with a hole in his sock.*

Give her another few pounds and explain how grateful we are.

FRANCIS *reads.*

PENROSE. Is that what Daddy would do?

FRANCIS. It's what I used to do on his behalf.

PENROSE. Oh hell. You know how she finds me a little odd...
the way I sleep on in the day... so I hardly see her from one
morning to the next. You know confidence deserts me when
I'm tired out... how I get nervous and can't be myself.

He picks up his glass, drinks, and then blows down the straw.

FRANCIS. Penrose, don't do that, it's very annoying.

PENROSE (*putting the glass down*). Yes. (*Making a hole in his
sock.*) You're kind to me in my dreams at the moment...
when I manage to catch a few hours' sleep, that is, because
for some particular reason, that I can't particularly fathom, I
stop worrying about you for those few hours... but that
doesn't include tonight when I was worrying about you
rather a lot... all day... all this week... all this year gone by,
since we put Daddy in the soil and I threw the rose you had
given me onto his coffin, and Mrs Nicholson cried. You're
quiet as a church mouse, Francis. Why do I sense you're
unhappy? (*Waits for an answer.*) It's somehow more hurtful
now that Daddy isn't here and you've taken his chair. (*Waits
for a response.*) Can I ask a question... a thousand queries
probably... what am I doing wrong? At one time you would
have told me. I've tried to think what you would say... hear
your voice... listen to your advice... when I'm tossing and
turning in bed all night long... but even in the small hours
you're silent. I want your help.

His sock comes off. He puts it back on.

You talk about fairness. What is fair when you treat me like
this? I'm young and gullible, I realise that. Perhaps I'm
irresponsible in some ways... and need your guidance to
grow up a certain extent. Might I be right about this? (*Waits
for an answer.*) Your silence is punishing me. I'm so sorry...
if it's deliberate... I really dislike you for it. If it's not
deliberate... then I hope you know I'm here to help... at
least to listen... if you think I'm too hare-brained and
immature to help. We're brothers, you and me.

FRANCIS. We're not brothers, Pen.

PENROSE. Yes, we are. We always were, and we always will be as far as I'm concerned.

FRANCIS. I'm not your brother.

PENROSE (*blocking his ears*). I don't want to hear this.

FRANCIS. You're not my brother. I'm the gardener. I'm the man who does odd jobs about the house, who keeps it ticking over.

PENROSE. Poppycock... is what you used to say to me. (*Twisting the neck of his T-shirt.*) I'd be making up a fabulous story as we walked home from school... or you were getting my beans on toast. I adored the idea of a lovelorn prince in a castle cut off by the tide.

FRANCIS. It isn't my fault you can't sleep.

PENROSE. No.

The neck of his T-shirt gets a hole in it. FRANCIS *refills his glass and drinks some wine.*

I loved the idea of a Holey Island in Northumberland letting in the rain.

FRANCIS. Yes.

PENROSE. I remember all the stories you told me... the one about the giant who blew out and sucked in to make the tides. (*Twisting the hole in his T-shirt.*) Francis... I've been meaning to ask you... no, that's not exactly right... I've been meaning to let you know... and I apologise... if I've got this wrong... and I'm all muddled up in my ideas... I say sorry to you all the time... at least to myself... when I'm counting sheep in bed... but you don't know me as you think you know me... I change a little... day by day... experience by experience... as we all do. I'm not quite the boy you think I am... not quite so odd... or young... and, Francis... yes, you mend things about the house... but I want to ask you to leave them broken from now on... because... you know this as well as me... you'd be very good... no, that's not quite accurate enough... I wish to get this perfect... you would be a star, Francis... just as Daddy was a star at The Old Bailey... if you were to go back to school… old as you are… to study… and take all the necessary exams… to become a doctor… or a teacher… or whatever it would please you to be.

FRANCIS *scratches his knee.*

FRANCIS. No.

PENROSE. Why?

FRANCIS. It isn't going to happen.

A slight pause.

PENROSE. Why?

FRANCIS. It isn't something I'm going to do.

PENROSE. Why?

FRANCIS. I like you best when you're somewhere else in another room and not a pest.

A slight pause.

PENROSE. Why?

A slight pause.

FRANCIS. You make me feel guilty sometimes.

PENROSE. Why?

FRANCIS. You just do.

PENROSE. Well, it would please me most if you were a teacher.

A slight pause.

FRANCIS. It's been difficult since Daddy died.

PENROSE. Yes, terrifically hard. (*Picks up his glass.*) By far the worst year of my life.

He blows down the straw.

FRANCIS. I'm sorry.

FRANCIS *gets up and takes his book back to the shelf.*

I can't write, Penrose.

PENROSE. Pardon?

FRANCIS. Yes.

PENROSE. Why?

FRANCIS. Question after question.

PENROSE. You can.

FRANCIS. No.

PENROSE. I've seen you.

FRANCIS. You haven't.

PENROSE *thinks*.

PENROSE. No, you're absolutely right.

FRANCIS (*embarrassed and looking away*). I could barely read
    when I came here. At school, who wore the fool's cap?
    (*Looks back.*) As a boy I was pathetic in a way. I did have
    opportunities. When Mummy asked me to read to you at
    bedtime I was ashamed to say I couldn't, so I sat on the edge
    of your bed and made up stories that fitted the pictures, and
    watched you drift off to sleep night after night. As time went
    by, and you'd started school, I asked you to read to me with
    your finger under the words. I picked it up from you. Don't
    you remember?

PENROSE. No, and I've a brilliant memory. I can think of us
    reading together upstairs or in the kitchen by the fire.

FRANCIS. What was I doing?

PENROSE. It's a good job I was an excellent reader or we'd
    both be imbeciles. I'm absolutely flabbergasted. I've always
    been tickled by secrets.

FRANCIS. You showed me how to use a dictionary. (*Takes an
    old dictionary off the shelf.*) I found this in two volumes.
    Thousands upon thousand of words, all ready and waiting.

PENROSE. It's thoroughly shocking I didn't know.

FRANCIS. We all have secrets, Pen. However familiar we are
    with someone else, we still have secrets. I'm sure you have a
    few hidden away somewhere.

PENROSE. If I have it isn't deliberate.

FRANCIS puts the dictionary on the floor and another book on top of it, and another, and another.

I'm terminally dumb.

FRANCIS. I'm very good at secrets.

FRANCIS stands on the pile of books and reaches up for another one.

I found your father extraordinary, the way he was able to think and write so quickly with an old, scratchy fountain pen.

FRANCIS sits down with the book and reads. He drinks wine and refills his glass at the same time.

PENROSE (*playing with his sock*). You were brought up in Northumberland?

FRANCIS. Yes.

PENROSE. Why?

FRANCIS. Why were you brought up in London?

PENROSE. I was just checking.

A slight pause.

Mummy and Daddy were here.

A pause.

What are you reading?

FRANCIS. It's about a boy, who murdered another boy, in the 1910s, and the case was appealed. The boy had a very low IQ. (*Lowers the book to show a handwritten note.*) For some reason your grandfather has marked it. (*Goes back to the book.*) It's an obvious mistake. He threw a lump of wood and it caught the other child on the head. The case hinges on the previous two hours when the boys were fighting over a halfpenny stick of liquorice. The appeal was dismissed. Your grandfather is clearly outraged.

A pause.

PENROSE *picks up his glass and blows down the straw.*

A pause.

PENROSE (*making a hole in his sock*). Are you frightened?

A slight pause.

FRANCIS. Frightened of what?

PENROSE. I don't know.

A slight pause.

Yourself.

FRANCIS. Penrose, don't get philosophical; it's too late in the day.

PENROSE. Have you brothers and sisters?

FRANCIS. Only you.

PENROSE. Parents somewhere?

A slight pause.

Did you love Daddy?

FRANCIS. Stop bothering with it all.

PENROSE. I didn't, if I'm completely truthful. (*Making holes in his socks.*) Daddy had a soft spot for you. When did he ever tell you what to do, or advise you on how to do it... about the garden? He kept his own counsel on almost everything... including me. Only when he was dying was he wise... and generous. I think as a child he found me annoying, with my girly likes and dislikes... my liking for fairy stories, which... as it turns out... you were making up as you went along. You talked to him more than I was allowed to... when on so many evenings... after Mummy died... you were invited in here for a glass of wine. (*Gets up and goes towards the shelf of books.*) Daddy was gregarious on occasions, I know such, when he was talking about the law and had a difficult decision to make... an adjudication to give. (*Begins to put the books on the floor back on the shelves.*) I know all this because I was listening at the

keyhole... after my bath... in my pyjamas... when you both
thought I was in bed. Or the door would be ajar... and I'd
catch a glimpse of him... explaining something important
about the law to you... standing here... where I am now.
And to be quite honest, Francis, I was rather jealous. He
never quite understood me or knew who I really was... I was
an idea to him... he had ideas for me... about who I would
be... what I would achieve... particularly in court... he had
in mind I'd be a lawyer... since more than anything else he
wanted me to be like him... without ever particularly telling
me so... when I would be entirely hopeless in court.

*He knocks out the books that he has put back on the shelves
and they clatter to the floor.* FRANCIS *turns and* PENROSE
looks down. FRANCIS *gets up and puts the books back on
the shelves.*

FRANCIS. What's the matter with you, Pen?

PENROSE *shrugs.*

PENROSE. Nothing.

FRANCIS. It's something.

PENROSE. Are you jealous, Francis?

FRANCIS (*looking away, briefly*). Who of?

PENROSE *shrugs.*

PENROSE. I don't know.

A slight pause.

Me? I was wondering if you were jealous of me.

FRANCIS. Why would I be jealous of you?

PENROSE. I don't know.

A slight pause.

I asked because I think you might be.

PENROSE *knocks out two books and they clatter to the floor.*

A slight pause.

I'm truly sorry, that was bit much of me and very offhand.

FRANCIS. Yes, it was.

FRANCIS *picks up the books and puts them back on the shelves.*

PENROSE. Why are you unhappy?

FRANCIS. I'm not unhappy.

PENROSE. Is it my fault?

FRANCIS *goes to his chair. He drinks wine and pretends to read.*

FRANCIS. Come and sit down.

PENROSE *shakes his head.*

You didn't embarrass yourself. Stop looking silly.

PENROSE *wanders to his chair and sits.* FRANCIS *plays about in his nose, finds something and flicks it towards him.*

PENROSE. Missed.

FRANCIS *pretends to read.*

I'd love to visit Northumberland and see your childhood places.

FRANCIS. Would you?

PENROSE. I know we won't.

FRANCIS. It isn't going to happen, Penrose.

PENROSE. I am allowed to care about you. (*Twists his hair round his fingers.*) It goes about my head, Francis… forgive me… that you're not always honest about your feelings… no, that's not quite right… it's that you cover up by omission… the little deceptions are in what you don't say rather than what you do.

FRANCIS *closes his book and puts it on the small table.*

Funny things, brothers, I imagine… falling into friendship… falling out of friendship… the small, hurtful things that go on within families. If you ask me what I longed for most in this world… absolutely most… the paramount thing… it would be to have had a brother. You were sixteen when you came and I was a small boy of two. All too often love is a helpless thing. I read about it in novels. I haven't fallen in love with a girl yet. Unfortunately for me it hasn't come along. It's part of my sadness. It isn't that I love you in an ordinary way... in a bookish way... not, that would be wrong... you're too crooked for that. I can't find you in a book. I can't remember a time when you weren't here. You were my family... when Mummy and Daddy were preoccupied elsewhere... which was sometimes the case for days on end. I don't know why I had a tantrum just now. It's the first time I've done that in my life, and I'm sorry. (*Looks at some hair that has come out in his fingers.*) I can't find our relationship in a book. (*Puts his hands in his lap.*) I can't remember a time when I didn't trust you, even though... I've come to realise... you don't always tell the truth. You falsify and invent... fabricate very cleverly. Once upon a time I was fooled by your stories. Even now you're trying to show nothing on your face... something that gives you away... and you're very good at it. Why? Why haven't I asked you about this before? (*Waits for an answer.*) If it's my turn and I'm embarrassing you, or you feel uncomfortable, jolly good, so be it. I may even sleep tonight... though I doubt it... I believe sleep is a thing that will elude me for ever... whilst I'm troubled. This is not easy for me, Francis... but you know that. I know there is something making you miserable. I'm speaking candidly... when I don't know what there is to be candid about... except you're lonely. It's so strong I can almost hear it. It's like a shout. It's a cry for help. I hear it again and again. It's in what you don't say rather than what you do say. It's why I asked you if you were frightened.

Waits for FRANCIS *to respond. Gets up and goes to where his father used to stand.*

You killed a bird once, you told me. With a bow and arrow you had made. The arrow knocked its head off, you said. And yet the bird's heart was still beating, when you picked it up. You told me you felt guilty... but not until some years later... if I'm remembering correctly. And I want to ask you: how long did its heart beat for? How closely did you look at it?

Did it lie nestled within the palm of your hand… in your twelve-year-old fingers… without its head? And what were you thinking? You must know the answers to these questions, Francis. Did you then eat the bird feathers and everything? This is how your story went. And you were driven to a hospital… taken in a car because you lived in the wilds of Northumberland… but who was with you is a mystery… your mother… or your father? (*One of his legs shakes a little*.) You were in hospital for four days… and they had to remove it from near your liver… the chaffinch… because it had somehow found its way there… without disintegrating… and was still intact… without its head. And you were ill for a while, quite under the weather. And everyone thought you were a strange child… including the doctors… not because you'd swallowed a chaffinch, but because you thought it was funny… and asked to eat it again… but the bird had been thrown away by then… incinerated… and you wouldn't be consoled… so you became quiet. Quiet quiet quiet, to get revenge. You were a murderer, you told me. (*Wonders if* FRANCIS *will respond*.) And I was frightened for a very long time… not frightened of you, but of the story… a little bit of you because you told the story… and I wondered, even when I was ten years old… when we were grooming Pluto, who had caught a goldcrest… why you wanted to frighten me. Had I done something grotesque… been naughty in some way… and it's only now… not quite this second, but in the last few months… I've come to the conclusion that you enjoyed frightening me… and I say this because you still do it from time to time. And, Francis, I want to ask you why? (*Waits for* FRANCIS *to say something, his leg shaking*.) Is it because we're a family, and families can be envious? Or jealous, as brothers are jealous of one another sometimes… I suppose… I wonder?

A slight pause.

FRANCIS. Go to bed, Pen. It's getting late.

PENROSE. No, I'm not sleepy.

FRANCIS (*getting up and going to the desk*). I've ears. I hear what you say.

PENROSE (*his leg is shaking*). Yes.

FRANCIS *looks at the photographs.*

FRANCIS. There were photographs of you all over the house. (*Picks one up.*) The naughty faces you pulled when a camera came out. The impishness of you. The mischievous you. (*Puts it down and picks up another one.*) In this one you're standing on your head. You were going through that period when you did everything upside down. I remember you trying to eat jelly the wrong way up. (*Puts it down and picks up another one.*) You were a beautiful child, Pen. Adorable from head to toe. I wasn't. I was hideous.

PENROSE. Why don't I believe you?

FRANCIS. I learnt too much too soon about ugliness.

PENROSE. Yes... I expect so... if you say so.

FRANCIS. You were happily cherished.

PENROSE. Was I? Perhaps I've forgotten.

FRANCIS. When Mummy and Daddy were busy for a few hours, I did the cherishing, as a brother might have done. (*Flings the photograph across the room onto the chair where* PENROSE *was sitting.*) There were no photographs of me. No one ever asked me. I don't think a single photograph of me exists. Go to bed before I get really angry and break something.

PENROSE (*quietly*). Oh hell.

A slight pause.

PENROSE *goes quickly.*

FRANCIS. Where are you going?

PENROSE. To get a camera.

FRANCIS. Don't be so stupid.

PENROSE *stops.*

A clock in the house chimes midnight.

PENROSE *goes*.

A slight pause.

FRANCIS *picks up the photograph and puts it back on the desk.*

PENROSE *has a sponge cake with lit candles, a knife, and a large white envelope attached to a helium-filled balloon by a ribbon.*

PENROSE (*entering, singing*).
Happy birthday to you,
Happy birthday to you,
Happy birthday, dear Francis,
Happy birthday to you.

He puts the cake on a small table.

FRANCIS. Where did the cake come from?

PENROSE. I baked.

FRANCIS. Where did you get the recipe?

PENROSE. Off the internet.

FRANCIS. I'm gobsmacked.

PENROSE. Blow out the candles.

FRANCIS *blows out the candles.*

Cut it. It's your cake.

FRANCIS (*cutting two slices*). Where did you get the ingredients?

PENROSE. I shopped for them.

FRANCIS. You, went shopping?

PENROSE. I can shop, Francis. I'm not completely idle.

FRANCIS *tries the cake.*

I'm worrying it might be soggy in the middle. I don't know if I baked it long enough?

FRANCIS. It's delicious.

PENROSE *eats cake.*

PENROSE. I was worried I'd gone berserk with the sugar, since it refused to stay in the bag and went all over Pluto, who was on the table helping. When you were hideous, did you bake?

FRANCIS. No. I'd have baked with you, like we played conkers.

PENROSE. Don't you eat heaps of cake up in't north of England?

FRANCIS. You're such a Londoner, Pen.

PENROSE. I'm not as it happens.

FRANCIS (*licking his fingers*). You love being cosseted. You're a Londoner through and through.

PENROSE. I don't eat eels.

FRANCIS. That's a different part of London. This is Highgate. You're the wealthy part of London.

PENROSE (*licking his fingers*). Daddy had eels for breakfast.

FRANCIS. Yes. It made him think he knew about the world and was able to judge it fairly.

PENROSE *picks up the envelope.*

PENROSE. Happy birthday.

FRANCIS *opens the envelope and peers inside. He pauses for a moment.*

FRANCIS. What is it?

PENROSE. It's papers and deeds. I want you to have the house, Francis, as a present from me. It rightfully belongs to you.

FRANCIS *takes the deeds from the envelope and looks at them.*

It is now mine to give, by the way.

FRANCIS. Yes.

PENROSE. I've been to see Daddy's solicitor. We'll need to do it properly, sign the papers over. I'm not a dunderhead.

FRANCIS. I've never thought you were.

PENROSE. I can deal with life when I absolutely must do.

FRANCIS. Yes.

A slight pause.

PENROSE. I've been so worried about this moment.

FRANCIS. Why?

PENROSE. I was nervous you'd say no and go nuts.

A slight pause.

FRANCIS. I might go nuts in a minute.

PENROSE. I told you I was worried.

FRANCIS. Daddy left it to you.

PENROSE. It's property. The oldest brother always inherits the property.

FRANCIS. It wasn't left to me. Everything in the will went to you.

PENROSE. It was an oversight on his part, which I'm putting right.

FRANCIS. How much is the house worth?

PENROSE. Who's bothered? It's a place to rest our heads and bake cakes on Sunday.

FRANCIS. It's worth millions, Pen. How on earth am I meant to keep it ticking over?

PENROSE. I've thought of that. (*Takes a cheque from his pocket.*) Happy birthday.

FRANCIS (*looking at the cheque*). This is a fortune, for goodness' sake.

PENROSE. It's money. Who cares in this world about money?

FRANCIS. You will, when there's none of it left.

PENROSE. There's millions more. Now can you see why I've been lying awake at night, tossing and turning on soaked-through sheets?

A slight pause.

FRANCIS. This is wrong.

A slight pause.

PENROSE. I'm worrying less. I'm thinking you're going to accept. Am I right to be optimistic?

A slight pause.

FRANCIS. No. Be pessimistic.

PENROSE (*blocking his ears*). I don't want to hear this. I really am not going to listen, Francis. It's not equal and it's not fair… and you really are going to accept. (*His leg starts to shake.*) Otherwise you can go and get out, this second, and I will not have anything to do with you ever again.

FRANCIS (*putting the deeds in the envelope*). It isn't what Daddy wanted. I wasn't a beneficiary.

PENROSE. It's not his money.

FRANCIS. It is in a way, Pen. It's family money, as some of it was left to him.

PENROSE. No. It's my money, left to me.

FRANCIS. What happens if you have a family one day?

PENROSE. I won't.

FRANCIS. Are you sure?

PENROSE. Yes.

FRANCIS. You don't know, unless you're a fortune-teller.

A slight pause.

What if I was to sell it and run off to the south of France?

PENROSE. Why are you so difficult?

FRANCIS. I'm being realistic.

PENROSE (*walking away*). I hate you for this, by the way.

FRANCIS. You don't hate anyone and probably never will.

PENROSE. I might do one day, I'm getting enough practice.

He picks up the book he was reading and throws it at the wall.

FRANCIS. And don't have a tantrum.

PENROSE. I'm not having a tantrum. You have tantrums.

FRANCIS. There's a reason for mine. I'm not lucky like you.

PENROSE *takes a packet of Gauloises from his pocket and lights a cigarette. He runs his fingers through his hair.*

(*Going to him.*) You're setting yourself on fire. (*Taking the cigarette and putting it out in an empty glass ashtray on the desk.*) Mummy died of lung cancer.

PENROSE *goes to the shelves and knocks out two or three books.*

Happy now?

PENROSE. Much happier, thank you.

FRANCIS. I've not seen anything quite so childish since you were four.

PENROSE. You've not been looking. (*Knocks out a book.*) Don't tell me what I did when I was young... or how you liked me best when you would pick me up at school and I was playing hopscotch with the girls... or knitting. I'm tired of hearing it. You're not Daddy or Mummy. (*Knocks out a book.*) You're the odd-job man, so be satisfied. (*Another book.*) You're treated very well here. (*Another book.*) It's the best job in London. (*Another book.*) I don't know what the problem is... we would still be together? (*Another book.*) We could still do the things we always do? (*Another book.*) Is that the problem? Don't you want to do them any longer? (*Another book.*) Am I being taught some kind of lesson... about standing up for myself?

A slight pause.

It's my life.

FRANCIS. Nobody's life is completely their own, Pen.

A slight pause.

PENROSE. It's my house.

FRANCIS. Yes.

PENROSE. Why won't you take it?

FRANCIS. I can't.

PENROSE. Yes, but why?

FRANCIS. It belongs to you. We all have responsibilities, you to me and vice versa. Mine is to you and your family. (*Looks at the books*.) To your history if you like, to this house, and the years to come.

PENROSE. Why are you being so unkind?

FRANCIS. I'm not.

PENROSE. So ungracious and callous?

FRANCIS. I'm not.

PENROSE. You're a terrifically big teller of lies.

FRANCIS. I'm sure you're right.

PENROSE. And not very good at it for someone who thinks he is.

A slight pause.

I'm sure you were, once upon a time, very good at it indeed.

A slight pause.

I loathe you intensely at this second, and if I knew how to hurt you I would.

FRANCIS. No, you wouldn't. It isn't in you.

PENROSE. Is it in you?

He goes to the door.

(*Stopping*.) Just to let you know, I will be forging your signature.

FRANCIS. I can't write, Penrose.

PENROSE (*stumped briefly*). With an 'X'.

PENROSE *goes.* FRANCIS *is still and tries to compose himself. He picks up a photograph, looks at it, and then thumps it with his fist, breaking the glass.*

PENROSE *plays the piano in the music room.*

FRANCIS *empties the bottle of wine into his glass and drinks. He picks up the envelope and cheque, and puts them neatly on the chair where* PENROSE *was sitting. He sits in his chair and sprawls with his legs over the armrest, and looks at the tiny amount of blood on his fist.*

FRANCIS (*suddenly singing and joining in with the song* PENROSE *is playing*).
>   By a lonely prison wall, I heard a young girl calling:
>   Michael, they have taken you away,
>   For you stole Trevelyan's corn
>   So the young might see the morn.
>   Now a prison ship lies waiting in the bay.
>
>   Low lie the fields of Athenry
>   Where once we watched the small free birds fly
>   Our love was on the wing
>   We had dreams and songs to sing
>   It's so lonely round the fields of Athenry.
>
>   By a lonely prison wall, I heard a young man calling:
>   Nothing matters, Mary, when you're free
>   Against the famine and the crown,
>   I rebelled, they cut me down.
>   Now you must raise our child with dignity.

PENROSE (*singing solo at the piano in the music room*).
>   Low lie the fields of Athenry
>   Where once we watched the small free birds fly
>   Our love was on the wing
>   We had dreams and songs to sing
>   It's so lonely round the fields of Athenry.

As PENROSE *has been singing,* FRANCIS *has gone to the books and started to pick them up.* PENROSE *plays on. One by one* FRANCIS *is putting the books back onto the shelves.*

FRANCIS (*suddenly singing as* PENROSE *continues to accompany him*).

> By a lonely harbour wall, she watched the last star falling
> As the prison ship sailed out against the sky
> For she lived to hope and pray
> For her love in Botany Bay.
> It's so lonely round the fields of Athenry.
>
> Low lie the fields of Athenry
> Where once we watched the small free birds fly
> Our love was on the wing
> We had dreams and songs to sing
> It's so lonely round the fields of Athenry.

The piano goes silent. FRANCIS *picks up the novel* PENROSE *was reading and puts it neatly with the envelope and cheque.*

PENROSE (*somewhere in the house, calling*). Goodnight.

FRANCIS (*calling back*). Goodnight, Penrose.

He sits in his chair and does nothing but think.

ACT THREE

A few weeks later.

A trig point on a hill in the Northumbrian countryside. A metal-grey sky with a shaft of sunlight through it. A storm is coming across the fell and autumn settling in. There is the sense that FRANCIS *and* PENROSE *are on the roof of the world. The younger man should not be wearing soft shoes, but he is, and has a bag on his shoulder.* FRANCIS *goes to the concrete trig point and climbs on top while* PENROSE *is nonplussed, blinks, and wishes he was in London.*

FRANCIS. You're unusually quiet.

> PENROSE *looks at him as if to say can we go home.*

About here are some of the best walks in the country. You enjoy walking.

> PENROSE *blinks several times.*

This is one of my childhood places. Just here. This very spot. I'd come on foot or the bike. I'd chuck it over fences if I didn't go on the tractor tracks. The ride down was faster, bumping over the stones. I came up here to scare myself an' pretend I was lost.

> PENROSE *looks at him.*

We'll use the gates going back so you don't 'ave to climb over so much.

> PENROSE *looks in his bag.*

What're you looking for?

PENROSE. My iPod.

FRANCIS. It's in the car. You left it in the car.

PENROSE. Oh.

FRANCIS. What's up?

PENROSE. I didn't think there'd be so many fields with dangerous sheep in them waiting to pounce. You were meant to show me where you lived.

FRANCIS. I lived here.

PENROSE. Your house, near a pleasant café or theatre. I didn't expect to climb many of the highest peaks in Britain.

FRANCIS. One. An' it's not a peak. This is Executioner's Hill.

PENROSE. I'm treading on blood as well as dung. Why did those bullocks follow us like the Gestapo?

FRANCIS. It's what young cows do.

PENROSE. On the way back, tell them I don't eat beef.

FRANCIS. They'll know from your odour. Cows have good noses.

PENROSE. You're thoroughly enjoying every minute of this.

FRANCIS *looks down into the valley.*

FRANCIS. If you'd bother to use your eyes, you'd see where I was brought up.

FRANCIS *points.* PENROSE *looks.*

Can you see the pouncing sheep?

PENROSE. I'll ignore that.

A slight pause.

I can see white animals.

FRANCIS. Come round t'your right, there's a farmhouse with two chimneys, one smoking, then a lane, bordered by a line of trees, going into a wood. On the edge of the wood is a great house, you can't miss it, with a terrace, an' a lawn sloping down to a lake, with an island an' gazebo. The house has eight gargoyles. There are seventy-one windows. If we were down there and looking this way, we wouldn't spot us. See it?

PENROSE *takes in the size of it.*

PENROSE. Yes. Crumbs.

FRANCIS. It's Castlewhistle Hall. It was built in the 1870s by Lord Castlewhistle from Newcastle. He sent coal down the Tyne to London and beyond. He dug the lake an' planted the gardens from moorland. I worked out he needed more than a million tons of soil. Prince Albert is said to 'ave come here to play croquet, and lost. It's where I was brought up.

PENROSE turns and looks at him.

Yer think I'm one thing only t'find out I'm something else.

PENROSE. Yes.

PENROSE looks at the house.

FRANCIS. The house has forty-one rooms and thirty-nine fireplaces. I counted 'em. Three oak staircases. On summer days we'd play rounders on the lawn. All of us kids. We weren't meant t'go in the lake, but did when no one was looking, in our pants. We'd kick plaster off the walls in the gazebo, when their backs were turned because a child was crying.

PENROSE (*quizzically*). Your brother?

FRANCIS. No.

PENROSE. A sister?

FRANCIS. No. Keep guessing.

PENROSE looks at the house.

PENROSE. A children's home.

FRANCIS. Yes.

PENROSE looks down.

Don't get upset, yer silly sod.

PENROSE. I'm not.

A slight pause.

I'm sad.

A slight pause.

I'm thinking of the story of the boy playing rounders, who hit the ball so hard it went round the world and hit him on the nose.

FRANCIS (*looking at the house*). I thought yer knew in a way.

PENROSE. No.

FRANCIS. It was a brilliant place t'live. I had all this land. I thought it was mine, as far as the eye can see. I knew it weren't, but in my head it was. I owned the trees.

A slight pause.

PENROSE. Why does it still matter quite so much?

FRANCIS. It doesn't. It was a long time ago.

PENROSE. I can tell it's still so crucial.

A slight pause.

FRANCIS. Yes.

PENROSE *looks at the house.*

PENROSE. Look at the house, Francis, and tell me what you see.

FRANCIS. I don't 'ave your imagination.

PENROSE. You don't need it. You lived it. I wish to know.

FRANCIS *looks at the house.*

FRANCIS. I can't.

PENROSE. I can see raggedy children playing football, with jumpers as goalposts. Are you the goalie? Or the young boy, with a girl, embracing behind a tree? There's an adult and a child. A woman with a boy. She's being overly sympathetic... her sympathies are false, she doesn't really mean it... but she's doing her job. The boy is crying, he is hurt. She is resentful... perhaps she wants to get off home... to her own children. The boy has scruffy hair, grey flannel, school shorts and cut knees... scuffed shoes. Is he you? Did you feel unloved? Is that why you loved me so much? (*Waits for a reply, but doesn't get one*.) The boy and girl are kissing… you're a few years older, perhaps… in the woods. And even though you're kissing, you're lonely and frightened. Forgive me… courage… courage… courage… I've always known I'm an oddity, not quite like other men, not the ordinary man I might wish to be… but neither are you… with your quirks… and smoke screens.

FRANCIS *scratches his knee*.

FRANCIS. You're very young.

PENROSE. Am I?

FRANCIS. No one is ordinary, Pen, if we know them well enough. Least of all you, least of all me.

He looks at the sky.

There's a storm coming. We're goin' t'get wet.

He gets down off the trig point.

PENROSE. I wonder if… when you were a boy… you didn't get soaked to the bone and really enjoy it… on your own… the magic of it. Did you pick flowers in the fields about here? Mmm? Cowslips and celandine?

FRANCIS (*looking at the sky*). It's goin' t'tank it down any minute.

PENROSE *takes an old conker on a length of string from his pocket*.

Where did yer find that?

PENROSE (*apologetically*). Well… they hunt in the countryside… so I read about… foxes and hares, poor things… so I went hunting in your room.

A slight pause.

FRANCIS. Did you?

A slight pause.

PENROSE. I do apologise.

A slight pause.

FRANCIS. You bloody cheat. You fucking sneak. Yer'd no fuckin' right.

PENROSE (*stepping back and looking down*). No. I'm sorry. It was in a biscuit tin.

FRANCIS. I know what it were fuckin' in.

PENROSE. Yes. Cleverly hidden away.

FRANCIS (*grabbing the conker*). Not cleverly enough, fuckin' obviously.

A slight pause.

Yer little shit.

A slight pause.

This was a twenty-oneser.

PENROSE. Pardon?

FRANCIS. A twenty-oneser. It means it beat twenty-one other conkers.

He throws it at the trig point. PENROSE *goes to pick it up.*

Don't pick it up.

PENROSE. You may still want it.

FRANCIS. I don't.

PENROSE *stops.*

What else did yer come across, in yer little treasure hunt?

PENROSE. Nothing. (*Sheepishly looking down.*) I didn't really find anything else.

FRANCIS. Don't lie to me, Pen. Don't ever fuckin' lie to me.

PENROSE *puts his bag on the grass and takes out a piece of paper with a pressed flower on it.*

PENROSE. It's a celandine.

FRANCIS. I know it's a pissin' celandine. Give it me.

PENROSE *shakes his head slightly.*

I won't ask again.

PENROSE. You'll destroy it and it's gorgeous.

FRANCIS. It's mine t'destroy, yer fuckin' baby.

A slight pause.

PENROSE. No. You're not having it.

FRANCIS. I'll fuckin' thump yer.

PENROSE. Do it.

FRANCIS. I pissin' will.

A slight pause.

PENROSE. No.

A slight pause.

You might have done once, but not now.

A slight pause.

I think you were the one who was hit, not the hitter. You couldn't fight back. It's why you came up here to be on your own, away from the other children... who teased you because you pressed flowers. Francis, you wear a shell like a tortoise.

He looks at the flower and puts it back in his bag, takes out an old biscuit tin and opens it. It is empty apart from a penknife, an old photograph, and an envelope. PENROSE picks up the penknife and looks at it. He gives it to FRANCIS. FRANCIS looks at it and puts it in his pocket. PENROSE picks up the photograph.

A photograph. (*Giving it to him.*) How old were you?

FRANCIS (*looking at it*). I don't know. Thirteen or thereabouts.

PENROSE. You've a cigarette dangling from your lips, so no more disapproving faces, please, when I smoke. No more motherly looks.

FRANCIS gives him the photograph.

You were an attractive boy, ever so insouciant, with your never-washed face.

He puts the photograph in the tin and picks up the envelope.

(*Looking at the envelope.*) There's a drawing of a woman. Your mother? And squiggles, meant to look like words. What does it say?

He gives the envelope to FRANCIS *who looks at it.*

Inside is a page torn out of a catalogue, of table lamps.

FRANCIS *takes out the torn page.*

FRANCIS. When I was eleven, I thought, when I see 'er again, I'll give 'er a lamp.

PENROSE. Did you?

FRANCIS (*shakes his head*). No.

PENROSE. How old were you?

FRANCIS *holds up both hands and then a finger.*

Eleven.

FRANCIS. Yes.

PENROSE. When she left you on your own?

FRANCIS. Yes.

A slight pause.

I was here five years.

PENROSE. Why, Francis?

FRANCIS. I don't know why. She musn't've loved us, Pen. Some mothers don't love their kids. They get in the way. They're a nuisance. All I know is she left us locked under the stairs at Christmas, for a week. I couldn't get the door open. (*Touches his leg.*) I broke this foot kicking. I wasn't strong. I was a weak kid. It was dark. No light at all in the night, a line of it round the door in the day. An' freezin' cold. There was no toilet, nowhere t'piss, or do the other. All there was to eat was raw potatoes. My gob got so ulcered it was like a monkey'd shat in it.

He scratches his knee. PENROSE *goes to the conker and picks it up. He gives it to* FRANCIS.

Thanks.

FRANCIS *scratches his knee.*

Are you all right?

PENROSE *nods.*

PENROSE. I'm thinking of knitting trousers for frogs.

FRANCIS *scratches his knee.*

FRANCIS. The neighbours 'eard us crying on Christmas Eve.

PENROSE. You said us?

FRANCIS. I meant me. Jus' me. The police smashed their way in, took the fridge away that was blockin' the stairs door. Grabbed us an' pulled us out, with the 'ead teacher of the school in a turquoise coat. She'd come with a packet of chocolate buttons. It's why I like chocolate.

PENROSE *takes a conker from his pocket.*

PENROSE. I brought mine. I don't know what age of oneser it is. You didn't tell me about that.

FRANCIS. Your go.

They play conkers.

She'd went off with her latest boyfriend, 'adn't paid the rent. She was an 'eroin addict... I don't know, Pen. I know she took from shops. She was Irish, from Dublin originally. Mebbe she went back there. My dada was Irish. She'd tell us 'e was a gypsy, a tinker, with a caravan... lived by the side of the road. Some days 'e were from Cork, other days from Galway, but 'e always 'ad an 'orse and a bad temper... in 'er stories about 'im. Them were the good days, when she'd tell us about 'er life in Ireland. As a girl, growin' up in Dublin, they'd kept a pony in the flat. How she'd got from there to 'ere, I don't know. How she got to Manchester an' Timperley... an' why... I don't know... except as a boy, growing up 'ere, I used to think about it a lot. I'd imagine stuff about Ireland, wondering if she came because of me, if I'm really Irish. I 'ad a nose full of snot. A kid growing up in these hills... always wondering... always fuckin' wonderin' about everything. Why I came 'ere, Pen, I don't know either.

Why they put me in a car an' drove me, miles away, I can only wonder about. Except I'm 'appy they did. (*Puts his conker in his pocket.*) I win.

PENROSE. I always lost.

FRANCIS. Yes.

PENROSE *blinks*.

A raisin dropped in a glass of Champagne will continuously bounce up an' down from the bottom of the glass t'the top.

PENROSE. Why didn't you go to school?

FRANCIS. I did.

PENROSE. Where?

FRANCIS. Manchester. Here, if I didn't get off the bus first.

He looks at the sky.

It really is goin' t'bucket it down.

He scratches his knee.

I did petty things wrong, opportunistic things. I took an old lady's purse once. She jus' 'appened to put it down in a shop. If a saw a chance, any chance, a took it. A bit of smashing car windows f'the fun of it. I set fire to a tree, which didn't go down well, in Timperley. Mind you, I was pretty drunk. All this 'appened with me mam. By the time I got 'ere I'd no friends... an' was a lot better off because of it.

PENROSE *blinks*.

PENROSE. Did you go to prison?

FRANCIS. No. Little lads don't go t'prison. I 'ad a kindly judge one time... somethin' like Daddy.

PENROSE *blinks*.

PENROSE. Did he know, Francis?

FRANCIS. Know what?

PENROSE. All about you.

FRANCIS. Yes. 'E asked me an' I told 'im. Yer dad was clever. He'd years of practice, 'e'd 'ave spotted a lie a mile off. He changed my life, Pen. Literally in a moment he changed it, with an act of kindness.

PENROSE. What?

FRANCIS. He put my wages up.

A slight pause.

PENROSE. Yes. Did he ask you not to tell me?

FRANCIS. Yes, he did.

PENROSE. You should have told me.

FRANCIS. I hate myself for doin' it now.

PENROSE. You should have broken the rules.

FRANCIS. No. Never. Never again.

PENROSE *bends down, makes sure everything is back in the tin, and puts it in his bag.*

Tin's mine.

PENROSE (*putting the bag on his shoulder*). I'm keeping it safe for you.

FRANCIS. Am I being told you're fed up?

PENROSE. You're being told it's going to rain.

FRANCIS (*walking about, looking for something*). I know these fells an' the weather like the back of my hand. We've a good few minutes yet. (*Picks up a twig.*) I was known as Frank round 'ere, by the other kids. An' Frankie-boy by the farmer I used t'go an' milk cows with, when I was skipping school. (*Takes his penknife from his pocket and cuts the ends off the twig, leaving it straight to make an arrow.*) Or puttin' up a fence, or on a ladder fixin' the gutter on the barn roof. I 'ad my own little garden at Castlewhistle. Jus' down from the kitchen window. It was a few feet by a few feet. I used t'cut the lawn with scissors. The cook would watch us, weedin' an' stuff with a spoon. One year she gave us bulbs t'put in f'the spring.

PENROSE. I'd love to go there. Why don't we go?

FRANCIS. No.

PENROSE. We could.

FRANCIS (*sharpening one end of the arrow*). It's an 'otel. It's why I left, why I 'ad to pack me bags. I was sixteen, 'ad to go in any case, no skin off my nose the place shut.

A slight pause.

PENROSE. I'm sorry.

A slight pause.

FRANCIS. Yeh, I was an' all, Pen.

PENROSE (*looking at the house*). Where was the farm you milked cows?

FRANCIS. Castlewhistle Farm, yer lookin' at it.

PENROSE (*pulling a face*). I'd be frightened I'd hurt them.

FRANCIS (*cutting a notch in the other end of the arrow*). You wouldn't.

PENROSE. Wasn't it smelly and slithery?

FRANCIS. There were only two of 'em. You 'ad to milk 'em by 'and.

PENROSE. It's cruel to steal from an animal. I wouldn't want my udders fingered. It's definitely barbaric. (*Blinks innocently.*) I'll have to stop having milk on cereal.

FRANCIS. It doesn't leave you very much to eat.

PENROSE. And write to the *Guardian*. In fact you can write. It can be your first challenge.

FRANCIS (*picking up another twig*). No.

PENROSE. Why not?

FRANCIS. I'm too old.

PENROSE. Too lazy. What are you doing?

FRANCIS (*cutting the ends off the twig to make a bow and stripping away the bark*). Yer'll see soon enough.

A clap of thunder rumbles across the hills from quite a few miles away.

PENROSE *looks into the distance.*

PENROSE. I know I'm going to get soaked.

FRANCIS. Yes.

PENROSE. Must I get flu?

FRANCIS. Afraid so, Pen. I need one of the conkers.

PENROSE *puts his bag on the ground.*

PENROSE (*taking the tin from his bag*). Which one?

FRANCIS. Any one.

PENROSE (*offering him the conker*). You can have mine.

FRANCIS. Give us a few seconds.

FRANCIS *continues to make the bow.* PENROSE *watches him. He blinks.*

PENROSE. Why did you go to London?

FRANCIS. Are your questions on a list, or coming t'yer gradually?

PENROSE. On a list.

FRANCIS (*works on the bow for a moment*). They gave us a few quid. I spent it on a train ticket.

PENROSE. Were you on your own?

FRANCIS. Course I was, daft 'alfpenny, daft sod. Who else would be with me?

A slight pause.

PENROSE. I know you've brothers and sisters.

FRANCIS. 'Ow come you would know that?

PENROSE. I just know.

FRANCIS. Do you?

PENROSE. Yes.

FRANCIS. 'Ow come?

PENROSE. I know you.

A slight pause.

FRANCIS (*cuts a notch in one end of the bow*). I 'ad a sister. A little sister.

PENROSE. Where is she?

FRANCIS. She died when we were under the stairs.

PENROSE *blinks.*

PENROSE. Oh hell.

A slight pause.

Oh hell.

FRANCIS (*cutting a notch in the other end of the bow*). I didn't care for 'er as I should. I tried, but it wasn't enough.

A slight pause.

He puts the bow on the ground and picks up the arrow.

(*Stripping the bark from the arrow.*) I went to London t' get away from the whole bloody thing.

A clap of thunder rumbles across the hills from the distance.

There are things yer just do, an' I just did it. It wasn't a plan. I've never 'ad a plan.

PENROSE. I'm truly sorry, Francis.

FRANCIS. Of course you are.

PENROSE. How old was she?

FRANCIS. There's no point in asking, Penrose, really. She was seven-and-a-half.

A slight pause.

I'd enough money left over f'a room f'a month, found this crummy bedsit in Archway, ran by a couple of drunks, who'd got a stuffed Pekingese on the sideboard. I 'eard about a job, gardening, with a room t'go with it. Mebbe I expected t'stay a few months, I don't know. I didn't have a plan. Yer don't 'ave plans if yer brought up like me. Yer drift. Plans are for educated people.

A slight pause.

PENROSE. Where is she buried?

FRANCIS. I don't know, Pen. I didn't get to go to her funeral.

PENROSE. We have to find out. It's so important you find her and see her grave.

FRANCIS. Yeh, maybe it was once.

PENROSE. I'll help you.

A slight pause.

FRANCIS. I always wondered if she 'ad an 'eart attack or something, but I don't know.

PENROSE. What was she called?

FRANCIS. It don't matter, Penrose. It was an Irish name. If it's all right with you, I'll keep some thoughts to myself? Not everything 'as to be shared.

PENROSE. Yes.

PENROSE *pulls a face.*

FRANCIS. Don't look so concerned. Yer see why I 'ate it when you ask questions. All I do then is feel guilty. (*Puts down the arrow, picks up the bow and continues to work on it.*) I preferred you when you were young, didn't cheat, an' go sneaking about in my room. When I put you into bed, switched out the light, or took you to ballet class in the car. How it all 'appened I don't know. It wasn't a plan. I loved it when yer dressed up, trailed about downstairs in Mummy's shoes, without a care in the world. Forgive me, now an' again these memories are deliberate. It's a rest from it all.

The sky darkens. A crack of thunder echoes around the hills.

PENROSE. It's about now I wish I'd packed a mac.

He touches FRANCIS *on the arm.*

Thank you.

FRANCIS. What for?

PENROSE. I think you know what for.

A slight pause.

You're so clever at covering up.

FRANCIS. Am I?

PENROSE. I hope you'll say when I'm too much.

FRANCIS. I 'ave said, I will say, I do say. You're not too much.

PENROSE. I do know myself, quite well.

FRANCIS. I know you do, Pen.

PENROSE. I'm tougher than you imagine. There's no need to mollycoddle me quite so much.

FRANCIS. It's all I know how to do.

PENROSE (*touching* FRANCIS *on the arm*). It's my fault for clinging on.

FRANCIS. It's not your fault.

PENROSE. I have to let you go.

A slight pause.

FRANCIS. Conker.

PENROSE *gives him the conker he has been holding all this while.* FRANCIS *cuts off the string.*

A crack of thunder not far away. The sky darkens.

(*Fastening one end of the string to the bow.*) It's not one of my best ones. I was better at it than this. It's pretty rubbish in fact.

He scratches his knee.

There was a time, up 'ere, Pen, one day on my own, when I thought: wow, no one actually cares. I should 'ave been at school, but there was a lovely freedom in it. I suddenly saw I didn't 'ave to care either. I could do owt a wanted, an' no one would bother, or even be aware. (*Bends the twig and ties the string to the other end of the bow.*) I killed a bird that day, which I told you about, with a bow and arrow. When you do stuff on yer own f'too long no one notices... they forget you... so I told them I'd eaten it, told 'em I could feel it flapping about, livin' inside me. It was the guilt that was flappin' about, I can tell yer. It was a fluke I'd 'it the bloody thing in the first place. It turned out it wasn't any kind of freedom, if we care about a bird. Or if we love somebody. It's more the opposite. To care about another person makes us uncertain. It makes us unsure. Love makes us think and it makes us worry. But at the same time it's better. The one thing I never did was give you a bow and arrow.

PENROSE *takes it from him.*

PENROSE. What do I do with it?

FRANCIS. You send the arrow off towards Scotland, if it doesn't fall apart.

FRANCIS *shows* PENROSE *how to use a bow and arrow as if they might be two boys.*

(*He says some of these things.*) Rest your hand there. Let the arrow settle on your fingers. Up a bit. That's it. Keep it steady. Look along the arrow. Take aim. It'll help if you close one eye. You're doing well. Find something to hit, don't worry, you'll miss it. You want the arrow to whoosh and fly. Pull the arrow back towards you and let it go.

PENROSE *sends the arrow towards Scotland.*

A flash of lightning. A massive crack of thunder rumbles across the top of the hill, and it starts to rain.

FRANCES *and* PENROSE *take in the sky.*

A flash of lightning. A crack of thunder so loud it might split the earth. The rain buckets down.

FRANCES *goes to the trig point and stands on it, raises his head so the rain catches his face, and in this moment is free.*

A shaft of sunlight comes out on hillside.

In the torrential rain, PENROSE *dances (like most things he does he is good at it) without a care in the world.*

A crack of thunder.

The interval.

ACT FOUR

Scene One

A few months later.

Rough ground at Highgate Cemetery. A wintry sunlight is filtering through trees, casting shadows on the weeds on a muddy bank and two headstones. One reads: 'Mary Collins. Writer. Journalist. Polemicist. 1958–2002.' Below is the inscription: 'I love you, Mummy, even when you're angry.' The other reads: 'Sir Trevelyan Penrose Collins. Father. Friend. Lawyer. Socialist. 1936–2012.' Beside the writer's headstone is an earthenware pot full of pencils and pens.

PENROSE *has his bag with him and a scarf, but hasn't bothered with a coat.* FRANCIS *is picking up a leaf or two and throwing them away.*

PENROSE (*taking his bag off his shoulder*). I went to The Red Hedgehog to see a play.

    FRANCIS *looks at him.*

    You asked me where I was yesterday evening and didn't listen when I told you.

FRANCIS. Was it good?

PENROSE. Yes, I enjoyed it.

FRANCIS. What was it about?

PENROSE. It wasn't about anything. We saw a boy and girl fall in love.

FRANCIS. Who did you go with?

PENROSE. Cordelia.

FRANCIS. Who's Cordelia?

PENROSE. She's a friend. She helps to put on the plays there. You could have come.

FRANCIS. I know I could.

PENROSE. You're always invited.

FRANCIS (*leaves cleared, looking at the headstones*). I've a tickle in my throat. I think I might be coming down with something.

PENROSE. It'll be the cold that's going about.

FRANCIS. I expect so.

> PENROSE *goes to his mother's headstone. He takes a card from his bag and stands it on the soil.*

PENROSE. Happy birthday, Mummy.

He goes into his bag again and brings out some pens and pencils. He takes old pens from the pot, puts the new ones in, and arranges them as if they might be flowers. He puts his hands together to pray like a boy at school.

FRANCIS. What are you doing?

PENROSE. I thought I'd say a prayer today.

FRANCIS. Please don't. Mummy wouldn't like it.

PENROSE. I thought I would on her birthday.

FRANCIS. She was an atheist.

PENROSE. Well, I'm not. I don't know how you know these things.

FRANCIS. Read her book *The Cost of God*. You'll be joining the priesthood next.

PENROSE. I'd love to be pampered by nuns... I can't think of anything more heavenly. Dear Lord, bless Mummy, bless Daddy, bless the cat now he's fifteen and getting on a bit, bless Francis and help him to understand he's not a scoundrel, though, as you know, it doesn't stop him behaving like one. Bless me if you can, and help me to be strong when I'm no good, and sexually unattractive and ugly and have no confidence because of it, except Cordelia doesn't think so, when really I'm worried, and joke about the Church to give a false impression and be slight, which is not me at all, but I do it because I'm shy and frightened of myself, and want to hide. You put these things into me, Lord, or Mummy did, or Daddy did, or Francis did. Lord, please help me to accept who I am, and Francis to acknowledge who he is. Lord, life has been hell since Daddy died a year and a half ago. And can we have pizza this evening, which I like and he hates, because he prefers all sorts of bohemian tapas-y stuff with balsamic vinegar and dead animals. And can you ask him not to go to the pub every evening.

FRANCIS. It's not every evening.

PENROSE. Without telling me where he's going, Lord, as it worries me and upsets me and I think I've behaved badly, which probably I have but I'm not certain.

FRANCIS. It's once or twice a week at most.

PENROSE. Lord, would you ask him if he will come to the concert tomorrow evening at the Albert Hall with Cordelia and me, and tell him he won't be a gooseberry. (*Waits for a reply.*) Lord, don't tell him that I've followed him down the hill to Archway because he enjoys the roughness of the pubs there, in particular Sweeney's, and sits at the bar all evening with his mates who build houses and drive buses, and are ex-army scaffolders. Don't tell him I've seen him drunk being sick in the gutter and on his shoes. Don't tell him I put him in a taxi one night, which he doesn't even remember, and only vaguely knew who I was. Don't tell him I've seen him pilfer money out of my wallet, when all he has to do is ask, or leave a note with a drawing of money on the kitchen table, and I'll get the message.

He gets to his feet and gives FRANCIS *one of his looks.*

FRANCIS. Grow up, Penrose. You're a little boy. A little boy who has everything. I'm sick to the back teeth of you. All you do is call out, and be ever so sensitive. Well, no longer. It's over. I'm not even angry any more.

PENROSE *looks down.*

I just don't care one way or another, who you're with, what you're doing, whether you're alive, whether you're dead. We musn't upset Penrose. Oh, no, we musn't make him cry. If you cry now I'll smash your face in. So don't even think about it. Delicate little boy. Delicate, what for? So you could get your own way. You've used it very cleverly over the years. Oh, he's so charming. Oh, he's so impish. Oh, he's so good at school. Sneaking into people's lives all the time. It's not what adults do, Penrose, it's what children do. Little boy, who can't, or won't grow up. How old are you? It's rhetorical so don't answer. I know it's your birthday tomorrow. The birthdays crowded in, didn't they? Mummy's and yours. Like a parent I know how old you are, you'll be twenty-three tomorrow, and not a day over six. I had got you a present. Well, you can put a bomb in the Albert Hall. If you want to go out with Cordelia, then go with her. It is, after all, what you've always done, to think about yourself first and not the family, to ask but not mean it, so we're an afterthought. I care less about you than a fly. The little boy with no feelings, the child without a heart. I love you, and then I stop loving you. I don't know how to describe it... I don't know what the metaphor is... for the love I feel for you. And you let me down, as love always does let you down, and I loathe myself. It's then I cry, quietly.

PENROSE *slowly looks up*.

PENROSE. Yes.

FRANCIS. What a terrible person you are.

A slight pause.

PENROSE. Yes.

FRANCIS. The little boy who's not once been hurt.

A slight pause.

PENROSE. No.

FRANCIS. What an empty person.

A slight pause.

PENROSE. Yes.

FRANCIS. Have you always crept about, since this is not the first time and I should have learnt by now?

PENROSE (*his legs shaking*). I used to go under the table when you were talking to Mummy in the kitchen, hidden by the oil cloth. Does that count?

FRANCIS (*angrily*). Yes, it does. What did you hear?

PENROSE (*gulps*). Nothing. You weren't often there. She'd be writing an article. It's not my fault she used to write in the kitchen. Even now, I wonder if she knew. I've no idea.

FRANCIS. Of course she knew.

PENROSE. Oh. She was at the table for hours. I'd be underneath it, and hungry. I'd take some little biscuits with me, and a cushion. I'd have my book to read. She didn't like small children. Especially silly boys like me. She'd shout a great deal.

There is an awkward silence between them.

FRANCIS (*quietly*). I wish you'd get out of my sight.

PENROSE. Yes.

A slight pause.

FRANCIS. I don't ever want to see you again.

A slight pause.

PENROSE. Yes.

FRANCIS. I think you heard me.

A slight pause.

PENROSE. Yes.

A slight pause.

FRANCIS. Why are you so forgiving?

PENROSE *goes to him and touches his arm.*

It would be so much easier if you threw me out. I used to live in fear of that.

PENROSE *takes a packet of Gauloises from his bag and puts a cigarette in* FRANCIS*'s mouth.*

PENROSE (*lighting the cigarette*). I know you smoke, Francis.

FRANCIS *smokes*.

You are coming to the Albert Hall by the way. I want you to meet Cordelia.

FRANCIS. Are you in love?

PENROSE. Don't be silly.

FRANCIS. That's what I say.

PENROSE. It's my turn.

A slight pause.

You're correct. I should have asked you before now, but I didn't do it on purpose. It's because I'm lackadaisical and scared these days. I'm very sorry.

FRANCIS. Sorry is something you have to mean, Penrose.

PENROSE. It won't happen again. (*His leg starts to shake.*) I thought I was doing what you wished me to, go off on my own, which is why I'm confused.

FRANCIS. Yes.

PENROSE. I wonder if you want me to be a different person, and that's not right. You're not my mother. You're not my father. You're a dear friend.

FRANCIS. Yes. I will get used to the idea. (*Smokes for a moment.*) It really hurts, Pen, when you lose a child. It's happened to me twice. Where does Cordelia live?

PENROSE. I don't want to give you the wrong impression, Francis; she's just a friend at the moment. I've to sort myself out, and do some serious thinking. I know we're good with each other. She's a bit kooky, but serious. I have to decide who I am and what I want. I haven't an inkling what she thinks as yet. She lives in Holland Park, so you'll know she's rich. Her mother is Celia Ormsby, the violinist. It's her concert tomorrow evening, playing concertos by Delius and Elgar. It is music you've listened to, or pretended you have and enjoy. (*His leg shakes.*) Francis, I think you've some serious thinking to do as well. About the house. It's falling down about our ears. There are so many mice, Pluto doesn't know where to turn. He's too old for it to be all his responsibility. When the guttering at the front falls on the postman we'll all be in court.

FRANCIS. Yes. I'll see to it.

There is an awkward silence between them.

How old is Cordelia?

PENROSE. She's the same as me.

FRANCIS. I wondered if she might be older, for some reason.

PENROSE. She's a few months older.

A slight pause.

I'm always going to look young. I hope so when I'm ninety. It bothers me sometimes. It's a struggle, when people imagine I'm this and that, when I'm not. It's bruising.

A slight pause.

How do you use a condom?

A slight pause.

FRANCIS. You put it on. You unroll it. You've got to buy one first.

PENROSE. Yes. When?

FRANCIS. When you're ready.

PENROSE. Yes. How will I know I'm ready?

FRANCIS. You just will. Stop worrying about it. Get her to put it on.

PENROSE. Yes.

A slight pause.

PENROSE *starts to leave*.

FRANCIS. Where are you going?

PENROSE. I need to pee.

PENROSE goes. FRANCIS watches him disappear into the trees.

He takes some pens from the pot and replaces them with new ones that have been hidden in his pocket.

PENROSE returns, but FRANCIS doesn't see him. FRANCIS hides the old pens, arranges the new ones and kisses the headstone. He becomes aware that PENROSE is there.

You're wearing new socks today.

FRANCIS. What?

PENROSE. I noticed earlier.

FRANCIS. What?

PENROSE. I've been meaning to tell you your feet smell of onions.

FRANCIS looks away.

I gave your old socks to the mice in the pantry. They're devoted to onions.

A slight pause.

If Mummy loved me, why didn't she say goodbye?

FRANCIS. She was finishing her book. I expect she was too busy.

PENROSE. Did you use a condom?

FRANCIS. What?

PENROSE. Did you and her use a condom?

FRANCIS. Penrose, don't be preposterous really.

A slight pause.

We should go. If we're going to walk to Parliament Hill.

There is an awkward silence between them.

I've not heard anything so ridiculous in a long time.

A pause.

I'll put more traps down for the mice. Don't you take them up this time.

A slight pause.

You can't have it both ways.

There is an awkward silence between them.

PENROSE. Where?

FRANCIS. Where what?

PENROSE. Where abouts in the house did you have intercourse with her?

A pause.

FRANCIS. I'll get someone in to mend the guttering and the roof.

A slight pause.

PENROSE. In their bed? In my bed? When I was out at school?

FRANCIS. Don't be silly.

PENROSE. In their bed.

A slight pause.

FRANCIS. You don't always have sex in a bed.

PENROSE. In the kitchen?

A slight pause.

In your bed?

A slight pause.

Where abouts?

A slight pause.

Who seduced who?

FRANCIS. I thought you were innocent.

PENROSE. Stop telling what I am… it's dangerous like a torn sail… I'm very angry at this moment.

There is an awkward silence between them.

Did Daddy know?

A slight pause.

It could be yes or it could be no. Those are the options.

A slight pause.

FRANCIS. No.

A slight pause.

PENROSE. You absolute cunt.

A slight pause.

Where abouts? In my bed?

FRANCIS. Once.

PENROSE. You absolute cunts, both of you.

A slight pause.

FRANCIS. It wasn't what you think.

PENROSE. What do I think, Francis?

FRANCIS. It was just once or twice.

A slight pause.

In the kitchen one time. A screw in the sink. It was just a few times. I wanted it to be more than it was.

PENROSE. Who seduced who?

FRANCIS. She seduced me.

PENROSE. Every time?

FRANCIS. Yes.

A slight pause.

It wasn't an affair. I wanted it to be, but it wasn't.

A slight pause.

PENROSE. Did she have affairs?

A slight pause.

Did she have affairs, Francis?

FRANCIS. Yes. I think so.

PENROSE. Did my father know?

FRANCIS. If he did, he didn't tell me. He wouldn't have told me in any case.

PENROSE. Was she cock-smitten?

A slight pause.

FRANCIS. Yes.

A slight pause.

PENROSE. Well, I forgive you a tiny tiny tiny tiny tiny tiny tiny tiny amount.

A slight pause.

Did you love her?

FRANCIS. Penrose, please don't ask.

PENROSE. Did you love her?

A slight pause.

FRANCIS. Yes. I liked the attention from someone like your mother.

A slight pause.

PENROSE. Well, you must have wept secretly the morning she died, whilst I was having a hissy fit. My father was in America... at Harvard... and had to come back. You all knew she had a lump on her lungs, whilst I refused to accept it, and wouldn't go to see her in hospital.

There is an awkward silence between them.

Did you use a condom?

FRANCIS. Does it matter?

PENROSE. It's on my mind.

FRANCIS. She saw to all that. I did as I was told. I always have, believe it or not. What are we doing now? We're doing what you want. Why are we going to Parliament Hill? You wanted the walk. All the horses I've backed have come in last. She wasn't a terrible person, Penrose.

PENROSE. No.

FRANCIS. One way or another we're all fallible, including you. I'm not perfect, though you expect me to be. Mummy wasn't perfect.

PENROSE. Yes. The tiny tiny tiny bit I forgive you is increasing to miniscule.

FRANCIS walks somewhere and stops.

Did she talk about me?

FRANCIS. Of course she did. She worried about you. When you were going through that period of putting your clothes on back to front we talked about you for hours. I told her it was your way of being funny.

PENROSE wanders to the birthday card and picks it up.

Don't rip it up.

PENROSE looks at the card.

PENROSE. No.

FRANCIS. It's what I would do, and feel guilty about it.

PENROSE (*putting the card on the soil*). Yes.

FRANCIS. I feel guilty most of the time.

PENROSE. Yes. I think I understand. What about?

FRANCIS. Everything. You. Your mother. The whole situation. Me. What I've done. What I've not done. What I should have done. Mostly you.

PENROSE. Why?

A slight pause.

Why?

FRANCIS. It's hard to say.

A slight pause.

PENROSE. Yes.

A slight pause.

Shall I say?

FRANCIS. No.

PENROSE. What was your sister called?

A slight pause.

FRANCIS (*quietly*). Bridie.

PENROSE. I didn't hear.

FRANCIS. Bridie. She was called Bridie. I let her down.

A slight pause.

PENROSE. No, you didn't.

FRANCIS. Didn't I?

PENROSE. No.

A slight pause.

FRANCIS. Didn't I?

PENROSE. You didn't let her down.

A slight pause.

You haven't let me down.

A pause.

FRANCIS. Thank you. It was worrying me. I didn't want to do the same thing twice. We should go to Parliament Hill.

PENROSE. In a minute.

A pause.

PENROSE *puts his bag on his shoulder. He joins* FRANCIS. *They leave towards Parliament Hill, where the day will draw in and the sun set.*

Scene Two

A few minutes later.

Parliament Hill overlooking London.

FRANCIS (*entering with* PENROSE, *who has a box of mint chocolates*). I liked you best when I used to pick you up at school and we'd come here to Parliament Hill, and I'd leave you dangling by your ankles upside down at the bottom of a tree whilst I climbed to the top. When it was snowy we'd come sledging.

PENROSE. I got attached to the world being upside down. I still am... everything is always the wrong way up. There might be nothing of me but I'm blessed, or cursed, with an elephant's memory, especially the scary speed of the toboggan.

They stop, and suddenly there is awkwardness between them. FRANCIS walks away and looks at the view.

FRANCIS. We should keep going. There's something about walking... I'm less self-conscious somehow.

PENROSE. I don't mind.

FRANCIS. What about?

PENROSE. Being embarrassed.

FRANCIS (*taking in the city*). London. I didn't think I'd be here this long. I thought a year or two.

PENROSE *takes in his city, where the shadows of the buildings, and of* PENROSE *and* FRANCIS, *are lengthening as the sun sinks in the sky.*

PENROSE. How can you have let Bridie down when you were only eleven?

FRANCIS. If you'd spent any length of time with your sister's body you'd know.

PENROSE *holds out the box.* FRANCIS *goes to him, takes a mint chocolate and eats it as he walks away.*

PENROSE. I go to pieces if I step on an ant.

A slight pause.

I'm not a man, whatever a man is.

A slight pause.

I'm too intimidated to be a man.

He holds out the box.

Too horrified.

A slight pause.

I care too much what people think.

He holds out the box.

It's a worry.

FRANCIS. You have the rest of them.

PENROSE. I worry all the time most people won't like me. I know I'm too easily bruised. I know I seem quite young.

FRANCIS. I was young for my age.

PENROSE. You still are.

FRANCIS. I looked young.

PENROSE. You still do.

A slight pause.

You're far cleverer than you realise, which is a wonderful thing.

A slight pause.

I don't know where my confidence went, but it's gone somewhere. I'm definitely a boy and not a man. I know I don't help. I learnt to play silly at school when everyone presumed I was gay. I've been doing silly ever since.

A slight pause.

It hurts, Francis. I can't get over myself somehow that I'm so unattractive.

FRANCIS *takes a step or two towards him.*

So unsexy and plain. I'm negligible. Who likes a boy?

A slight pause.

Cordelia tells me I'm attractive, but she tells me in a very unsexy way. She said I'm frightened of responsibility. It wasn't a seductive conversation. It hasn't been me somehow to love a girl in a sexy way, which is why I'm baffled and confused.

A slight pause.

We have good fun together.

He holds out the box. FRANCIS *takes a chocolate and eats it.*

It's courage I'm looking for... I don't know where it went... the trust I once had in myself. It's not you, Francis, in case you're thinking it is. I went through puberty too late, and there's the rub of the problem. I was mocked because of it. And shy because of it. You'd be surprised at the number of people who don't realise how shy I am. When I'm not with you I hardly say boo to a goose.

A slight pause.

I must seem naive when I have to ask you how to use a condom. I know it appears as if I flit over the surface of things. Why do people think I'm everything I'm not?

He offers FRANCIS *a chocolate.* FRANCIS *eats one.*

A slight pause.

What do I do?

FRANCIS *looks at him and walks away.*

You're not going?

FRANCIS. No.

PENROSE. Promise me you'll never go.

FRANCIS. I won't disappear like I did from Castlewhistle.

A slight pause.

PENROSE. I see your flaws... pardon.

A slight pause.

I wonder about Cordelia's and mine.

A slight pause.

Well... we're all damaged. But you, more than most people, deserve to be happy.

FRANCIS (*quietly*). Don't tell me that.

PENROSE. I didn't hear you.

FRANCIS. I said don't tell me that.

PENROSE *holds out the box.* FRANCIS *walks to the chocolates, takes one and eats it.* PENROSE *looks at the reddening sky.*

PENROSE. It will be evening soon. Can we please have pizza?

FRANCIS. Why are you so forgiving?

PENROSE. Why are you so forgiving, Francis?

FRANCIS. I'm forgiving because of you.

PENROSE *holds out the box.*

(*Looking in the box.*) There's none left.

FRANCIS *walks away.*

I won't come tomorrow night.

PENROSE. Why?

FRANCIS. You should talk to Cordelia.

PENROSE. I can do that whenever.

FRANCIS. All right. I'll come.

A slight pause.

What does she think of me?

PENROSE. She's not met you.

FRANCIS. What will she think of me?

PENROSE. She'll like you.

A slight pause.

Why shouldn't she respect you?

A slight pause.

I know you don't like yourself, but we'll put up with that for a few hours. (*Looks in the box and takes out a chocolate.*) You missed the last one.

He eats the chocolate.

FRANCIS. You should tell her what you feel.

PENROSE. Yes.

FRANCIS. What you told me, and don't be afraid.

PENROSE. I sort of have already.

FRANCIS. Whisper it whilst nibbling in her ear, but get naked first. There's nothing to having sex, Pen. It's just the confidence to have fun.

PENROSE. You sound like an expert.

FRANCIS. I wish I was.

PENROSE. Am I too vulnerable?

FRANCIS. No. Some women… girls… like that.

PENROSE (*thinks for a moment*). I understand.

He looks at the lights of city which are beginning to surround them.

Isn't love part of it?

FRANCIS. No, not in my experience.

PENROSE. Isn't it part of being a man, knowing how to love?

FRANCIS. I don't know, Pen. Ask me again when it's happened to me… apart from you.

PENROSE. Isn't it also part of being a man to let ourselves be loved?

A slight pause.

FRANCIS. Yes.

PENROSE *holds out the empty box.*

You had the last one.

A slight pause.

PENROSE. Some men find it difficult to do that.

A slight pause.

FRANCIS. Yes.

A slight pause.

I don't go to Archway to disappear. I go to the pubs down there to be alone amongst company. It's like anonymous sex with a prostitute. But you obviously didn't see that.

A slight pause.

PENROSE. I wondered, but I was too unsure to look.

A slight pause.

I was frightened.

A slight pause.

To love. To be loved. Difficult things.

A slight pause.

To be a pupil. To be a teacher. To learn. Difficult things.

A slight pause.

To listen. To change. To be better.

A slight pause.

To be responsible for another person. A difficult thing, Francis.

A slight pause.

FRANCIS. Yes.

PENROSE. It's a mighty thing, to be a parent.

A slight pause.

FRANCIS. Yes.

They are surrounded by the lights of London.

PENROSE (*looking at the city, almost turning in a circle*). The sodium lights of Highgate Village. The Olympic Stadium with the statue by Anish Kapoor, like a fairground helter-skelter. Canary Wharf, The Gherkin, the Dome of St Paul's, centuries old and just visible. The Shard, like a glass needle hurled into the earth from another planet. BT Tower which sends out messages across the globe. The broken tower blocks of West London. Richmond Hill, where at this time of year the deer are culled. We're here in the middle of it, on Parliament Hill. The greatest city in the world. If we were to shout from here it wouldn't hear us. (*Shouts.*) Hello. Hello. Hello. (*All he can hear is silence.*) It's unreal. It's utterly mesmerising.

ACT FIVE

A year later.

The lawn at 2 Old Highgate Road. It has stopped snowing, but the grass is covered with deep, newly fallen snow. The shadows of apple trees are being cast by the moon. The earth is in the grip of a cold and clear night.

FRANCIS *is wearing a cardigan and has bare feet. He holds out his arms and somehow manages to twist them together as if to make a rope. He hears* PENROSE *begin to play the piano in the house, which breaks the solitude.*

FRANCIS (*eventually turning, calling*). It's snowed all evening while you've been out. The garden is beautiful.

PENROSE (*calling from the music room*). I'll come and find you in a minute or two.

FRANCIS (*going like an old man closer to the house*). London doesn't know what snow is. Proper snow... not country snow, where the sheep get caught in the drifts. I used to help to dig them out. I can see their wool matted with ice even now. (*Looks at the garden.*) I once got lost in the snow at Castlewhistle. I should have been at school, but couldn't bear the thought of it. It was one of my useless days when I'd a scarecrow head. I lost my bearings in the snow. The things that made the landscape mine disappeared. I couldn't see the fences I knew like the back of my hand. I couldn't see the stone walls where I'd kept hidden bits and pieces. There were too many eyes at Castlewhistle... and thieving fingers. You weren't with your family. There wasn't the trust. (*Eventually he turns back to the house.*) I was telling you about the snow... about how I might have died when I was fourteen. I'd been out the whole day. There was something in me always wanted to find new places. Sadly the pleasure in finding out has gone from me now. (*Looks at the house.*) It had been snowing the whole day. There came the time... late afternoon as it was getting dark… when I suddenly realised I didn't know where I was. I had no idea where to go to get back home to Castlewhistle. It was snowing heavily. If I put my tongue out it turned to ice. It was getting in my eyes it was so heavy. The snow was stinging my eyeballs like a nettle. For the first and only time in my life I shouted out for help.

The piano goes silent.

I lay down and curled up in it. I lay down and made a ball in the snow… and it was warm like a holiday. Only once did we have a holiday from Castlewhistle when we went to Devon. We stayed on a houseboat at Salcombe, and caught mullet in the estuary. There were sailing dinghies… GP14s and smaller boats we could go solo in. We went to the beach in the sun. (*Looks at the house.*) You've stopped. Why have you stopped? (*Walks across the snow.*) Not long after I got up because I knew it wasn't true… something about being curled up in the snow nagged away, and I knew its warmth was going to kill me.

PENROSE (*entering with* FRANCIS*'s socks and shoes and a blanket*). Francis, come inside. Shoes in the porch. What on earth is all this?

He looks at him.

You're worse. I can see you're worse.

FRANCIS (*walking across the garden*). It might never snow again. It didn't snow last winter when we went to Parliament Hill, if you remember. I'm making hay while the sun shines. (*Takes a small tin from his pocket.*) I found this I'd squirrelled away. (*Opens the tin and takes out a tooth.*) Only a milk tooth thank goodness. You lost it one year while we were tobogganing down the hill and the rumpus when we couldn't find it in the snow… to begin with. It was a miracle we did. I didn't know you put teeth under pillows until you told me about the tooth fairy. Once a Castlewhistle boy, always a Castlewhistle boy. At school we were known, even by the teachers, as the Castlewhistle children. We were the ones who knew how to grab… the biggest piece of toast, the most cereal at breakfast, the largest potato… the prettiest book. I didn't do anything wrong. Nothing that can't be excused. I didn't damage or kill anybody. I picked the wild flowers in the hedgerows and fields before the sheep got to them, and didn't join a gang, thankfully. I didn't want to be in charge or be a leader.

PENROSE *puts the socks and shoes on the snow.*

I told you silly stories to frighten you... only little ones... only now and again... because I was jealous of you. I was a child myself when I came here. That's my crime, Penrose. It's all I ever did wrong. I deliberately hurt you with a few sentences of rubbish. (*Looks at the tooth.*) Or a ride down a hill too fast on a sledge. Yet somehow in my mind it's become magnified and massive in the last years. And I don't know why.

PENROSE *goes to him and puts the blanket round his shoulders.* FRANCIS *pushes it off so it falls in the snow.*

Why don't I deserve happiness when I've done nothing but good?

PENROSE *picks up the blanket, shakes off the snow, and puts it round* FRANCIS*'s shoulders.*

I'm still battling the demons I had when I was young.

PENROSE *kisses* FRANCIS *on the forehead.*

PENROSE. Your shoes and socks are there.

He goes towards the house.

FRANCIS. Where are you going? Is this you being brutal and cruel?

PENROSE. Yes. (*Stops and turns.*) It's as brutal as I'm capable of. I've asked you to see a doctor because you're ill. I can't fight your depression, Francis. You have to do that for yourself. Goodness knows I've tried to be generous, without success. (*Thinks for a moment.*) You're like a fly against a window, always trying to go somewhere but never going it. I think you need a stronger person and I'm sorry I can't be it. If I could be a different person, for your sake, I would become it. If there's anything I can do you know I will try. But I can't be who I'm not. I'd love to say sit down and I'll put your shoes on, but you won't let me. I will be so affectionate... if you'd allow me. (*Thinks for a moment.*) I think you do this deliberately, because you know I can't reply and answer back. If it's another story to frighten me, you're succeeding. (*Walks about.*) I'm pacing. I'm not going. I wish I could after the terrible evening I've had. (*Becomes still.*) This is not home. I think you should live somewhere else for a while. I think you should leave. I wonder if that wouldn't be best for both of us.

FRANCIS *looks at him.*

A slight pause.

FRANCIS. What will you do?

PENROSE. Well, I don't know... think and be peaceful. I tried inventing vegetarian cat food but Pluto wasn't excited.

A slight pause.

FRANCIS. What would you do with the house?

PENROSE. Sell it, even the mice have moved on. I've come to loathe the dark place. It's only the garden that keeps me here, and the garden keeps me here because of you. If we didn't have the garden, all these acres, our problems are over. Could you give up the garden?

A slight pause.

FRANCIS. No. I had plans for the spring. (*Walks across the snow like an old man.*) I had a few ideas to make an area for children, bigger than at Castlewhistle, where we could plant sunflowers and daisies, and I could watch them grow up.

A pause.

PENROSE. You've not asked me about my terrible evening.

FRANCIS. Go and play if you want. I'd like to hear you play.

A slight pause.

PENROSE. Your toes must be freezing.

FRANCIS. They're strangely warm. I can't fight this awful depression. There are days when I can't focus my eyes. It's beaten me, Pen. It's like being dragged underwater by an anchor. I know it's irrational, and selfish. I know I don't ask about you any more. I hope you won't sell the house because I want to clear the garden, in spring. There's so much to do to put it right. My head spins with possibilities. (*Walks across the snow.*) When Cordelia comes to live here I want it to be a place to sit in the sun.

A slight pause.

PENROSE. You hardly mention her, Francis.

FRANCIS. Yes. I don't trust women at the moment. It's gone from me. I don't know why. I've seen you holding hands and laughing together.

PENROSE. She makes me truly content. (*Looks down.*) I might go and play in a minute. It's been an appalling few hours. (*Looks up.*) Will you come inside, Francis?

FRANCIS. Go and play.

PENROSE. The world isn't always about you and what you want.

FRANCIS. I'd like to hear you sing.

PENROSE. No.

A slight pause.

It's the saddest evening of my life and you're not interested enough to ask why.

FRANCIS. The world isn't always about you, Pen.

PENROSE (*quietly angry*). Yes, and I learnt it tonight if I didn't know it before.

A slight pause.

FRANCIS. You're upset.

PENROSE. Yes.

FRANCIS (*walking across the snow*). I'm no good any longer. Why should I pretend to care when I'm not bothered one jot?

A slight pause.

PENROSE. I think you care as you always did.

FRANCIS. Why am I depressed?

PENROSE. I've grown up.

A slight pause.

FRANCIS. Is that why it is? I've nothing left to do except to look after the garden.

A slight pause.

What's happened?

A slight pause.

PENROSE (*shaking his head*). Nothing.

FRANCIS. Something's happened. Tell me.

A slight pause.

PENROSE. Cordelia's had a miscarriage. She's lost the baby.

A slight pause.

FRANCIS. Oh, Pen. When?

PENROSE (*a tear rolls out of his eye*). This evening. A few hours ago.

FRANCIS. Oh, Pen.

PENROSE. I'm really upset. (*Starts to go.*) I'm just going to the piano.

FRANCIS. Wait.

PENROSE *stops.*

PENROSE. Cordelia's inconsolable. I didn't know what to say to make it better.

FRANCIS. Where is she?

PENROSE. In hospital. They're keeping her in overnight.

FRANCIS. Oh, Pen.

PENROSE (*wiping his eyes with a handkerchief*). It's one of those things I suppose. It was awful, Francis. I felt so useless. There was nothing I could do. I even saw it. This little thing like a sack of blood and bits. A crumpled child. Dead. I somehow know she was a girl.

A slight pause.

I feel so guilty for some reason, as if it's my fault.

FRANCIS (*going to him across the snow*). You said it yourself. It's one of those things.

PENROSE. If we'd not gone to The Red Hedgehog it wouldn't have happened.

FRANCIS. It would have happened. You couldn't stop it. It's not your fault.

A slight pause.

PENROSE. The doctor kept looking at me as if was for the best.

A slight pause.

It was late for a miscarriage.

A slight pause.

Cordelia was stoical, actually, when the doctor was there. When she'd gone, Cordelia's breasts gave out tiny drops of milk. She was being a mother.

A slight pause.

I asked if we could bury the child, and they said we could.

A slight pause.

The loss is indescribable.

A slight pause.

I didn't need to ask if grief was normal.

A slight pause.

I don't know if I could ever be as brave as Cordelia is being. I don't know what will happen in the coming days, but I saw a mother who will care for a child come what may, and I'm lucky.

A slight pause.

FRANCIS. Yes.

A pause.

PENROSE. So are you lucky, Francis.

A slight pause.

FRANCIS. Yes.

A slight pause.

PENROSE. There was a young girl in the café, which was closed and dark with the safety lights on. It was a place to sit quietly while they got Cordelia settled in a ward, and I could go to her again. She must've been thirteenish, with parents who were old. They had a vacuum flask and biscuits. The girl had obviously had an accident a year or two ago. She was wearing a blue helmet and a harness, attached to a machine of some kind, and playing with a child's bendy toy. I don't know if she'd been knocked over by a car, but she was a child and would be for ever. She'd been robbed of being a woman. Her parents were dealing with her minute by minute, with a girl smashed up and left to live in her own head. I don't know why I should think of you, Francis, but I did, and it made me very cross. The girl had every reason to feel sorry for herself, lost in her own world, but of course she didn't. It was left to me to be sorry, watching across the empty tables, and to feel a little bit less sorry for myself.

A slight pause.

FRANCIS. Yes. (*Walks away across the snow.*) I know I said you weren't ready to look after a child. I want you to know I was hopelessly wrong. (*Turns.*) I feel ashamed as a matter of fact.

A slight pause.

PENROSE. Yes.

FRANCIS. You would look after a child really well. It's not losing you that hurt me, Pen. I've not lost you, I know that. It's the sense of atonement that hurts. I've made up for Bridie's death, but I still can't forgive myself. And I don't know why.

PENROSE. Yes.

FRANCIS. The loss of a child is the most powerful thing, in some of us. In these minutes, you must know how difficult it is. (*Lifts his head.*) Suddenly I feel better. I know I shouldn't but I do, because you understand.

A slight pause.

PENROSE. Yes, I do.

A slight pause.

FRANCIS. How long were you there?

PENROSE. What time is it now?

FRANCIS (*looking at his watch*). Nearly four o'clock.

PENROSE. Seven hours.

FRANCIS. You didn't ring.

PENROSE. I did. You didn't answer.

A slight pause.

FRANCIS. Have you had a drink?

PENROSE. There was a machine in the café, where the tea tasted like it was brewed in India and sent by pipe.

FRANCIS. Would you like something now?

PENROSE. I'd like you to put your shoes on.

FRANCIS. In a second or two.

A slight pause.

Did you ring Cordelia's mum?

PENROSE. Yes. In New York.

A slight pause.

Put your shoes on, please.

FRANCIS *walks and limps.*

Why are you so difficult?

FRANCIS. It's because I'm old.

PENROSE. How old are you?

FRANCIS. I want to be a hermit.

PENROSE. I'm not looking forward to you being old.

FRANCIS. I'm young. An infant.

PENROSE. Yes.

FRANCIS. Younger than you it would seem.

PENROSE *gives him one of his looks.*

I'm not important, Pen. Don't worry about me. You've enough to think about with Cordelia.

PENROSE. Yes. No.

FRANCIS. I must enjoy being like this, otherwise why would I be it.

A slight pause.

PENROSE. Yes. No.

FRANCIS. There's so much I don't understand. Can't understand. Won't understand. I'm not clever like you. (*Walks a few paces.*) I think if I do this, or do that, I'll be better. I do it, only to find out I'm not. I don't have your confidence. I wish I did.

PENROSE. You were confident. You are confident.

FRANCIS. No. It was a sham.

A slight pause.

PENROSE. Yes.

FRANCIS. I must get some kind of comfort from being like this, otherwise why would I be it? Yet it cuts like a scythe. It baffles me. Tell me what it is.

A slight pause.

PENROSE. I can tell you what to do.

FRANCIS. What?

PENROSE. Stop fighting. You're always fighting, Francis. There isn't an enemy.

A slight pause.

FRANCIS. No.

PENROSE. Once upon a time there might have been.

FRANCIS. Yes.

PENROSE. If there was, it's long gone. Stop it. Surrender. It's as if you're wearing a suit of armour when you don't need to. Next birthday I'm going to get you a Chieftain tank so you can live in it. (*Points.*) We'll chop down some apple trees and put it over there, with a bed in, soft and comfortable.

A slight pause.

FRANCIS. Yes. What else?

PENROSE. You tell me.

FRANCIS. I know what I want to be.

PENROSE. What?

FRANCIS. Free.

PENROSE. You can be.

FRANCIS. How?

PENROSE. I've told you.

FRANCIS. Yes.

PENROSE. Trust yourself.

FRANCIS. You told me to stop fighting.

PENROSE. That as well.

FRANCIS. Is there more?

PENROSE. Yes. One thing.

FRANCIS. Tell me.

PENROSE. Let me put your shoes on, as you once put on mine.

FRANCIS. Will you take care of me when I'm old?

PENROSE. You'll be in your tank protected from the world.

FRANCIS. I won't.

A slight pause.

You know what I'd like to be most of all? The gardener. I can't wait to watch the children grow up. I long to see you put them in the car; take them to piano and ballet, and to think I gave you the confidence to be good, when I didn't always have it myself. That would be freedom. You must go to Cordelia now.

PENROSE. In the morning.

FRANCIS. She needs you, Pen.

PENROSE. She's sleeping, I hope.

FRANCIS. Yes.

PENROSE *picks up the shoes and puts them on the snow by* FRANCIS.

PENROSE. You're tired.

FRANCIS. I'm lost.

PENROSE. Sleep will help.

FRANCIS. My head is spinning. I'm confused. I don't know what is true.

A slight pause.

I don't like myself.

A slight pause.

You shouldn't be thinking of me.

A slight pause.

PENROSE. Are you thinking of Bridie?

FRANCIS *nods.*

When she died, Francis, was she cradled in your arms?

FRANCIS *shakes his head*.

FRANCIS. No. She was in the corner.

A slight pause.

Will I ever be rescued from this depression?

PENROSE. Yes, because you owe it to her.

FRANCIS. I thought I owed it to you.

PENROSE. No. You owe it to Bridie.

FRANCIS. Yes, I do.

A slight pause.

Is there peace?

PENROSE. You can find it now.

FRANCIS. How?

PENROSE. Do you blame her, Francis?

FRANCIS. What for?

PENROSE. For not being strong enough to live?

A slight pause.

FRANCIS. Yes, I do. She left me alone.

PENROSE. You have to forgive her.

FRANCIS. I don't know if I can.

A slight pause.

PENROSE. Be wise. Do the clever thing.

FRANCIS. Yes, I see what you mean.

PENROSE. It wasn't Bridie's fault.

FRANCIS. She's made me angry all these years.

PENROSE. No more.

A slight pause.

FRANCIS. Yes, I understand. (*Walks away.*) For the first time I see why I'm angry. It can't go on, it has to end.

A slight pause.

I thought I couldn't forgive myself, but I was wrong.

A pause.

PENROSE. We should go in. I'm cold.

FRANCIS *goes to* PENROSE *and puts the blanket round his shoulders.*

FRANCIS. You go in. (*Walking away across the snow.*) I'll come in a few minutes.

PENROSE. I'll wait.

A slight pause.

FRANCIS. Is Cordelia coming here tomorrow?

PENROSE. We didn't get as far as talking about that. The house is icy, Francis.

FRANCIS. I know. I can fix it, but it will take a few days.

PENROSE. I had a go at mending the boiler.

FRANCIS. What did you do?

PENROSE. I banged it with a hammer.

A slight pause.

FRANCIS. Are you going to get married?

PENROSE (*shrugs*). Why would we?

FRANCIS. It's the traditional thing to do.

PENROSE. It's up to Cordelia.

A slight pause.

I think we'll go to Holland Park.

FRANCIS. Yes.

PENROSE. The boiler is beyond being repaired.

A slight pause.

FRANCIS. Shall I put a new one in?

PENROSE. If you would. Get an engineer in to do it.

FRANCIS. Don't you trust me?

PENROSE. He'll be quicker.

FRANCIS. I can do it.

PENROSE. I'll leave it up to you.

FRANCIS. Yes, sir.

PENROSE. Don't be ridiculous.

FRANCIS. No, sir.

PENROSE *looks at him quizzically.*

You might not want to be ordinary, but I do.

PENROSE *walks across the snow.*

PENROSE. Will you be in your tank when you're doffing your cap?

FRANCIS. I'm joking.

PENROSE *stops and looks at him.*

I'd be happy to be the gardener.

PENROSE. You've said.

FRANCIS. I'd be content with that, but you wouldn't. (*Takes off his cardigan.*) I'd be delighted to curl up in the snow.

He lays the cardigan on the snow.

I'm warm. I'm hot as toast.

PENROSE *goes to him and touches his shoulder.*

PENROSE. Your shirt is wet.

FRANCIS. I'm sweating.

PENROSE (*putting the blanket round his shoulders*). You could wring it out.

FRANCIS. My heart is going ten to the dozen, Pen.

PENROSE. You'll get pneumonia.

FRANCIS. I don't know whether I'm hot or cold.

PENROSE. Stop it. You're panicking.

FRANCIS. Yes.

PENROSE. Why won't you do as you're told?

FRANCIS. I never have.

A slight pause.

I'd cheerfully die.

A slight pause.

PENROSE *picks up the shoes and puts them beside the cardigan.*

PENROSE. You're not being fair.

FRANCIS. No.

A slight pause.

I'm sorry.

A slight pause.

PENROSE. How long have you been here?

FRANCIS. A few minutes before you came. I heard the car. I saw you sitting in it. I knew something was wrong. I thought it was the snow. I wondered if you'd had a skid on the hill.

PENROSE. The roads are treacherous.

FRANCIS. You go in. You've done what you can.

PENROSE. Have I?

FRANCIS. You've done all you can do. You've indulged me enough.

PENROSE. Yes.

FRANCIS. I know I'm self-indulgent. I can't stop it at this second. It's the way I am. (*Walks across the snow.*) I'm sorry I'm wrapped up in myself. Your being here isn't helping. We all think we can help, but we can't.

A slight pause.

As we talk, you make it worse.

PENROSE. Do I?

FRANCIS. I want to be the gardener.

PENROSE. Yes.

FRANCIS. You must let me be it. I can't ask more times than I have.

PENROSE. Yes.

FRANCIS. It's what I came here to be.

PENROSE. Is it?

FRANCIS. Leave my wages in an envelope on the kitchen table once a week and that will be enough.

PENROSE. I will if you'll be happy.

PENROSE *and* FRANCIS *look at one another.*

I'm scared.

FRANCIS. Why?

PENROSE. I just am. (*Walks across the snow.*) The plants do as they are told. Is that why you like them so much? There were no apples this year because of the frost in the spring which attacked the blossom. Winter into spring too soon, back to winter again. I do hear what you say. (*He is still.*) I owe you so much, but you have obligations to me. You owe it to me to be part of my family, Francis. I won't be putting your wages on the kitchen table, if you'll excuse me. I'm sorry, but I won't. I would if I thought it would make you happy for more than a year. I'm thinking of a lifetime. You have so much extra to give. I'm scared in case I'm wrong. It's the uncertainty that worries me, but that's life, isn't it? You're not old. You are incredibly young to be as silly as this. I offered you the house. Yes, it was done on a whim at the time... not quite a whim actually... but the offer is still there, if you've the courage to take it.

FRANCIS *twists his arms together as if he might be making a rope with them.*

Tell me what I felt the afternoon Cordelia told me she was having a child? Let me know how I was this evening. You wish to be in charge of the earth. You want to be in control of the soil. It's not the way it is for any of us. These curious things happen. I was of the view I could not be a father until a few hours ago, when I realised I could. (*Picks up the cardigan and takes it across the snow.*) Please. Francis, please.

FRANCIS *looks at him. He takes the cardigan and puts it on.*

A few snowflakes fall.

(*Looking at the sky.*) We could make a snowman with a carrot nose. My brain is porridgey tonight. I'm tired, we should go in. You're exhausted. I don't know what there is for breakfast. The bread is so mouldy it's dancing. If you want me to do anything I will do it.

FRANCIS *looks at him.*

We could build a tree house. I didn't have a house in a tree. We could picnic there this summer. Eat pig's trotters and jellied eels. Not me, but you. Did I tell you I'm thinking of learning the harp? I've an inkling you should do the same. The two of us. We could bully each other. The battle of the harps.

FRANCIS *gets down and starts to make a nest in the snow.*

Did I tell you I know what it is to be intimidated?

A slight pause.

Did I tell you I know what it is to be exposed?

A slight pause.

Did I tell you I know what it is to be defenceless.

He kneels down.

Please.

A slight pause.

Francis.

FRANCIS *closes his eyes.*

Stop.

He puts the blanket around him.

(*Singing*.)
> J'ai perdu mon Eurydice,
> Rien n'égale mon malheur:
> Sort cruel! Quelle rigeur!
> Rien n'égale mon malheur!
> Je succombe à ma douleur!

He gets up and goes to the shoes and socks.

Bringing them back.

> Eurydice, Eurydice,
> Réponds, quel supplice!
> Réponds-moi!
> C'est ton époux fidèle;
> Entends man voix qui t'appelle.

He blows into the socks.

It is snowing.

Putting FRANCIS*'s socks on him.*

> J'ai perdu mon Eurydice,
> Rien n'égale mon malheur:
> Sort cruel! Quelle rigeur!
> Rien n'égale mon malheur!
> Je succombe à ma douleur!

He starts to put the shoes on him and fasten the laces.

> Eurydice, Eurydice!
> Mortel silence! Vaine espérance!
> Quelle souffrance!
> Quel tourment déchire mon coeur!

He is still.

> J'ai perdu mon Eurydice,
> Rien n'égale mon malheur:
> Sort cruel! Quelle rigeur!

Rien n'égale mon malheur!
Sort cruel! Quelle rigeur!
Rien n'égale mon malheur!
Je succombe à ma douleur!
Je succombe à ma douleur!

It is snowing heavily.

The end.

A Nick Hern Book

A Breakfast of Eels first published in Great Britain as a paperback original in 2015 by Nick Hern Books Limited, The Glasshouse, 49a Goldhawk Road, London W12 8QP

A Breakfast of Eels copyright © 2015 Robert Holman

Robert Holman has asserted his right to be identified as the author of this work

'The Fields of Athenry' copyright © 1979 Pete St. John. Lyrics reproduced by permission. With acknowledgements and thanks to Pete St. John.

Cover photograph © Nobby Clark, with Andrew Sheridan as Francis and Matthew Tennyson as Penrose on Parliament Hill, London

Designed and typeset by Nick Hern Books, London
Printed in Great Britain by Mimeo Ltd, Cambridgeshire PE29 6XX

A CIP catalogue record for this book is available from the British Library

ISBN   978 1 84842 477 7